Sandra Lee
semi-homemade®

cooking 2

Meredith® Books Des Moines, Iowa

Copyright © 2005 Sandra Lee Semi-Homemade®. All rights reserved. Printed in the USA.

Library of Congress Control Number 2005921341 ISBN: 0-696-22715-0 Published by Meredith® Books, Des Moines, Iowa.

dedication

To my nieces and nephews, who are as sweet as candy and as sensational as souffle:

Scott, Danielle, Brandon, Austen, Stephanie, Taner, Brycer, Blakey, and Katie

May your lives be filled with love, joy, and all that is sweet!

– Aunt Sandy

special thanks

To all Food Fans, Food Fanatics, Food Purists, Food Enthusiasts, and Basic Foodies,

for living, learning and loving food—

May your lives be filled with fabulous flavor

acknowledgements

With much love and appreciation to my entire production and publishing family—

Jeff, Ed, George, Hilary, Wes, Angie, Lisa, Maryann, Pamela, Jules, Laurent, Robin, Linda,

Matt, Ashley, Jan, Mick, Amy, Erin, Gina, Jim, Jeff, Doug, Bob, Jack, and the entire Meredith Team

Thank-you for making our book so beautiful!

appreciation

To the following manufactures and retailers for their generous product contributions,

which helped to create the easy elegant look of Semi Homemade—

Room with a View, Vietri, Zrike, Love Plates, Fritz and Floyd, William Sonoma, Crate & Barrel,

Napa Style, The County House, F&S Fabrics, and Silk Trading Company.

Table of Contents

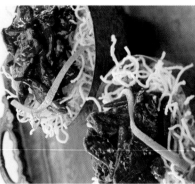

Introduction from Tyler Florence

As the host of Food Network's *Food 911*, I've had the chance to see first-hand what's really going on in the kitchens of everyday people. And it's consistent across the country—people have less time to cook but still want to put delicious, healthy meals on the dinner table for their families. Sound familiar? My friend Sandra Lee understands this dilemma and in this book provides easy, attainable solutions for you.

Sandra's book really addresses the needs of the everyday cook. Her recipes combine convenience products with fresh produce, meat, and dairy to come up with dinnertime solutions that are perfect for the time-starved cook. They are simple, fresh, delicious, and use products you probably already have on hand in your pantry. Her easy-to-follow recipes will help you get restaurant-quality food on the table in the comfort of your own home.

Like you, I love to cook dishes from around the world. In Sandra's book, you get ethnic at its best. From barbecue to Italian and Mexican to Asian, it's all here. Plus, the chapter on comfort food will bring back cherished childhood memories of Sunday-dinner meals—without the all-day prep.

I believe in the type of cooking that comes from a "real kitchen" and I know Sandra shares this passion. Her enthusiasm for good food is contagious and is evident in every recipe in this great book.

Enjoy!

Tyler Florence

Photo courtesy of Food Network™

Letter from Sandra

Growing up, I was known as the Bisquick® queen. As the oldest child of five, I cooked all the time, mixing up creative casseroles, thick, cheesy pizza and fresh-baked berry cobblers for my brothers and sisters. I wish I had that much time now!

No matter who we are or what we do, there are only so many hours in the day. I love preparing meals for those I love, but I don't want to spend my life in the kitchen. There are too many other things to do. Work. Play. Live. It's important to savor each precious moment with family and friends. This is why I created Semi-Homemade®—for you, your family and your friends.

My Semi-Homemade® philosophy is simple: start with 70% ready-made products, add 30% fresh ingredients, then take 100% of the credit for a dish or a dinner that's fast and fabulous! Substituting convenience products for labor-intensive ingredients lets you prepare delicious, made-at-home meals without "letting go" of taste. It's a new way of cooking for today's way of life.

Of the hundreds of recipes I've created, these are the ones I turn to again and again. Each chapter is a celebration of diversity—a tribute to the cuisine of Italy, Mexico, Asia and America that will have you cooking like the Global Gourmet. There are full-course meals and one-pot feeds all, dishes for everyday and dishes for special days, comfort food to cheer you up and health food to keep you fit. There are new favorites and old friends, foods we know and foods we crave, treats for kids and treats for adults.

Semi-Homemade® is completely stress-free. Each recipe is designed for one-stop shopping, combining straight-from-the-grocery shelves convenience with easy, step-by-step instructions and timesaving tips. Every single dish tastes irresistibly fresh and completely homemade. No one will ever know it's not from scratch. More taste for less work—that's a trade-off we can all enjoy!

With a warm hug,

Sandra Lee

A Helpful, Healthful Pantry

The more color in your diet, the more nutrients—so don't shy away from fresh produce. Look for fruits and veggies in their most convenient forms—prewashed, chopped, peeled ...

meats

prepackaged veggies

When purchasing canned
or jarred products be sure
to read labels and purchase
the items containing the lowest
levels of sodium, fat, and sugar.

fresh and canned produce

cheeses

peppers

13

A Helpful, Healthful Pantry

Whole grains are an important part of a healthful lifestyle. The new Dietary Guidelines for Americans recommend we eat three servings per day—and this shouldn't be hard to do as there are new products popping up every day on grocery store shelves.

pasta

white and brown rice

potatoes

nuts

Most of these pantry staples come in a time-saving form too. When you're in a race with the clock, use instant rice or couscous, prepackaged potatoes, refrigerated pastas, and prechopped nuts.

A Helpful, Healthful Pantry

From simple pot roast seasoning packets to dry salad dressing & soup mixes, these versatile seasoning blends make sensational sauces & gravies in seconds, adding new flavor to old favorites.

ground and whole spices

salt & pepper

coffee & tea

extracts & flavorings

Be adventuresome with spices—they don't add any significant calories and the right spice or seasoning can take a recipe from blasé to brilliant. Jazz up whipped topping with extracts or use coffee or tea as a no-calorie flavoring for savory dishes.

17

Italian

Fettuccine, risotto, pizza—Italian cuisine is America's most popular food. In Italy, each dish is prepared with unrestrained passion and a lust for living—and cooking. Fortunately, I've found a way to duplicate that robust flavor without spending my life in the kitchen.

From the light, delicate dishes of southern Italy to the heartier fare of the northern and central regions, this collection of recipes is as varied as the country itself. Mingling old-world flavor with new-world convenience, you can whip up a nutritious meal in the time it takes pasta to boil. You'll find everything you need for an alfresco feast: entrées, soups, salads and breads, and even a bread salad. Italian dining is about appreciating the food *and* the people sharing it with you, so go grande and invite your friends.

The Recipes

Sandra at her favorite store The Cheese Shop.

Tip: Italian foods are heavy on the garlic. After handling this potent bulb always wash your hands in cold water. It removes the smell, while hot water seals it in.

Creamy Phyllo Cheese Straws in Pesto

makes about 36 straws **prep time** 20 minutes **baking time** 12 minutes

- **1 package (8-ounce) cream cheese, softened, *Philadelphia*®**
- **1 egg, lightly beaten**
- **¼ cup grated Parmesan cheese, *Kraft*®**
- **¼ teaspoon salt**
- **1 box (16-ounce) phyllo dough, thawed, *Athens*® (40 sheets)**
- **1 stick butter, melted**
- **Store-bought basil pesto, *Buitoni*®**

1. In a small bowl, combine cream cheese, egg, Parmesan cheese, and salt. Mix well. Spoon cream cheese mixture into a resealable plastic bag. Set aside.

2. Preheat oven to 375 degrees F.

3. To use a resealable bag as a pastry bag, cut corner off bag to make a ¼-inch diameter opening. Lay out thawed phyllo dough. Working quickly to keep dough from drying out, brush top sheet with melted butter and pipe cheese filling along long edge of phyllo ½ inch from each end. Fold over ends to enclose filling and roll up phyllo to make a straw. Place straw on a baking sheet. Repeat with remaining sheets of phyllo.

4. Bake straws for 12 to 15 minutes or until golden. Serve straws with basil pesto for dipping.

Crispy Potato Pepper Cakes

servings 8 **prep time** 25 minutes **cooking time** 24 minutes

- **1 package (1-pound 4-ounce) shredded hash brown potatoes, *Ore-Ida*®**
- **1 red bell pepper, diced**
- **3 eggs**
- **1 cup shredded Parmesan, *Kraft*®**
- **1 tablespoon herbes de Provence**
- **Salt and pepper**
- **3 tablespoons olive oil, *Bertolli*®**
- **2 cups sour cream, for garnish**
- **1 cup finely shredded fresh basil, for garnish**

1. Preheat oven to 200 degrees F.

2. In a large bowl, combine potatoes and bell pepper. In a small bowl, beat eggs with cheese and herbes de Provence. Add to potato mixture and mix thoroughly. Season to taste with salt and pepper.

3. In a large skillet, heat oil over medium-high heat. Spoon a scant ¼ cup of potato mixture at a time into the skillet, pressing with the back of a spatula to flatten to a round about 3 inches in diameter (cook no more than 4 cakes at a time). Fry cakes for 2 to 3 minutes or until golden; turn and cook the other side until golden.

4. Transfer cakes to paper towels to drain. Transfer drained cakes to a baking sheet and hold in the oven. Repeat with remaining potato mixture. Serve topped with a spoonful of sour cream and sprinkled with shredded basil.

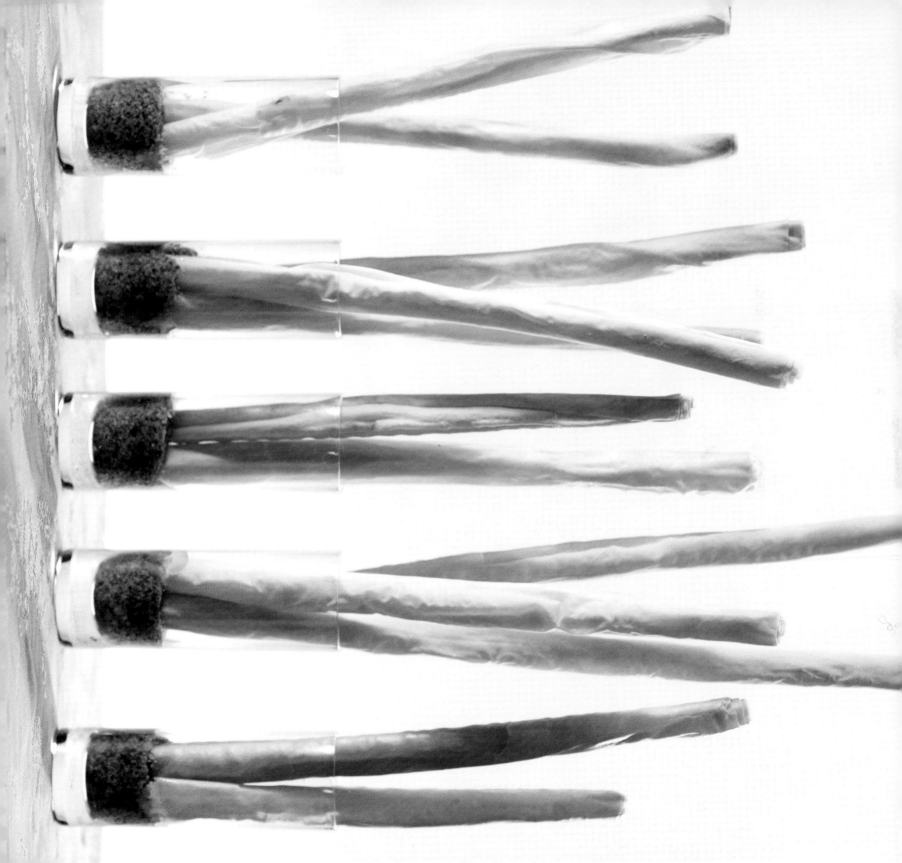

Minestrone Soup

- 1 quart low-sodium chicken broth, *Swanson®*
- 1 package (16-ounce) frozen garlic pasta with vegetables, *Green Giant®*
- 1 can (15¹⁄₂-ounce) kidney beans, drained, *S&W®*
- 1 can (14¹⁄₂-ounce) Italian-seasoned tomatoes, *Contadina®*
- ¹⁄₄ cup tomato paste, *Contadina®*
  Shredded Parmesan cheese, *Kraft®*

1. In a large pot, bring broth to boil. Stir in pasta with vegetables, beans, tomatoes, and tomato paste. Return to boil. Reduce heat and simmer for 5 minutes. Ladle soup into 6 soup bowls and sprinkle cheese on top before serving.

Garlic and Herb Focaccia

  All-purpose flour, for dusting
- 1 loaf (1-pound) frozen bread dough, thawed, *Bridgford®*
  Cornmeal, for dusting
- 4 cloves garlic, thinly sliced lengthwise
- 2 tablespoons extra virgin olive oil, *Bertolli®*
- 1 teaspoon Italian seasoning, *McCormick®*

1. Preheat oven to 400 degrees F.

2. On a flour-dusted surface, press or roll dough into a 12×9-inch rectangle. Transfer dough to cornmeal-dusted baking sheet. With a sharp knife, make 1-inch cuts randomly over top. Insert garlic slices into cuts. Brush with oil. Sprinkle with Italian seasoning. Let rise in warm place just until dough begins to puff a little, about 20 minutes.

3. Bake about 20 minutes or until golden.

Pesto
Pasta Salad

servings 4 to 6 **prep time** 5 minutes
baking time 9 minutes

1 box (14-ounce) cut fusilli, *Ronzoni*®
1 container (7-ounce) prepared pesto sauce, *Buitoni*®
¼ cup olive oil, *Bertolli*®
¼ cup white wine vinegar, *Heinz*®
2 cups cherry tomatoes, halved
 Salt and pepper
1¼ cups pine nuts, toasted
 Fresh basil sprigs, for garnish

1. Cook pasta according to package directions. Drain and rinse with cold water. Drain again and place in a large bowl.

2. In a small bowl, whisk together pesto sauce, oil, and vinegar. Pour over pasta. Add tomatoes and toss to combine. Season to taste with salt and pepper. Chill.

3. To serve, sprinkle with pine nuts and garnish with basil sprigs.

Bread Salad

servings 6
prep time 10 minutes

2 medium tomatoes, chopped
1 yellow bell pepper, stemmed, seeded, and sliced
½ cucumber, halved lengthwise, seeded, and sliced
½ small red onion, thinly sliced
1 tablespoon capers, rinsed, *Star*®
½ cup extra virgin olive oil, *Bertolli*®
¼ cup red wine vinegar, *Star*®
 Salt and pepper
2 cups garlic and herb croutons, *Marie Callender's*®

1. In a large bowl, combine tomatoes, pepper, cucumber, onion, and capers. In a small bowl, whisk together oil and vinegar. Season to taste with salt and pepper. Pour over vegetables and toss to combine.

2. Spread croutons in a single layer on a large platter. Spoon the vegetables evenly over croutons. Pour any remaining liquid in bowl over all.

Mini Cheese and Olive Calzones

servings 4 **prep time** 10 minutes
baking time 20 minutes

½ cup ricotta cheese
¼ cup shredded Mexican cheese blend, *Kraft®*
¼ cup chopped ripe olives, *Early California®*
1 teaspoon Italian seasoning, *McCormick®*
All-purpose flour, for dusting
1 can (8-ounce) refrigerated crescent-shaped dinner rolls, *Pillsbury®*

1. Preheat oven to 375 degrees F.

2. In a medium bowl, combine cheeses, olives, and Italian seasoning. Set filling aside.

3. On a flour-dusted surface, unroll dough in 1 piece. Press or roll out dough to a 16×8-inch rectangle. Using a pizza cutter, cut rectangle into eight 4-inch squares.

4. Place 2 tablespoons filling in center of each square. Lightly moisten edges with water and fold dough over to make a triangle. Seal edges by pressing with fork tines. Using the points of the fork, pierce vents in top of each calzone. Place on a greased baking sheet.

5. Bake for 20 minutes or until golden. Serve hot.

Roman-Style Artichokes

servings 4 to 6 **prep time** 10 minutes
cooking time 18 minutes

2 cans (8½-ounces each) artichoke hearts, *Reese®*
2 eggs
½ cup all-purpose flour
¼ cup yellow cornmeal
2 teaspoons Italian seasoning, *McCormick®*
1½ cups light olive oil, *Bertolli®*
Salt and pepper

1. Drain artichokes and pat dry. Cut in half lengthwise.

2. In a small shallow bowl, beat eggs. In another bowl, combine flour, cornmeal, and Italian seasoning.

3. In a small skillet, heat oil over medium-high heat.

4. Dip artichoke halves into egg mixture, allowing excess to drain off, then dip them into flour mixture, turning to coat. Drop a few at a time into hot oil. Fry until golden, about 6 minutes, turning once. Repeat with remaining artichokes. Drain on paper towels, season to taste with salt and pepper. Serve immediately.

Lasagna

servings 6 to 8 **prep time** 20 minutes
baking time 30 minutes

I've loved this lasagna since I was a child. My grandmother passed down the recipe and my sister Kimber, who won't share it with anybody, guards it closely. It's too good to keep to myself, so I'm passing it on to you. The unique flavoring comes from apple cider vinegar and health-conscious cottage cheese. Bake it two pans at a time—one to eat and one to freeze.

1 package (16-ounce) lasagna noodles
1½ pounds ground beef
1 medium yellow onion, finely chopped
2 cans (10¾-ounces each) condensed tomato soup, *Campbell's*®
2 tablespoons apple cider vinegar, *Heinz*®
1 tablespoon dried oregano, *McCormick*®
1 teaspoon bottled minced garlic, *McCormick*®
1 container (16-ounce) small-curd cottage cheese
1 package (8-ounce) shredded mozzarella cheese, *Sargento*®

1. Preheat oven to 350 degrees F. Cook noodles according to package directions. Drain.

2. While noodles are cooking, brown beef in a large skillet over medium heat; drain. Add onion, tomato soup, vinegar, oregano, and garlic. Simmer for 20 minutes.

3. Lay noodles lengthwise across bottom of a greased 13×9-inch baking dish. Spread a layer of cottage cheese over noodles. Add a layer of meat mixture, then cover with mozzarella cheese. Repeat for three layers. Finish with a layer of cheese.

4. Bake about 30 minutes or until bubbly and cheese is golden.

Italian Baked Pork Chops

servings 4 **prep time** 5 minutes
baking time 10 minutes

Mention Italian cooking and everyone automatically thinks of thick tomato sauce and melted cheeses, but the heart of Italian food is great cuts of meat, seasoned with a drizzle of olive oil and a savory blend of spices. Add a dash of Dijon mustard and a coating of crusty Parmesan. You then have a no-hassle main course in minutes.

1   tablespoon Dijon mustard, *French's®*
1   tablespoon extra virgin olive oil, *Bertolli®*
½   teaspoon Italian seasoning, *McCormick®*
4   pork center loin chops (6 ounces each)
     Salt and pepper
½   cup shredded Parmesan cheese, *Kraft®*

1. Preheat oven to 400 degrees F. Line baking sheet with kitchen parchment. Set aside.

2. In a small bowl, whisk together mustard, oil, and Italian seasoning. Season the pork chops with salt and pepper, then brush both sides of chops with mustard mixture. Press Parmesan into both sides of chops.

3. Place chops on prepared baking sheet. Bake about 10 minutes or until just cooked through.

Tip: Chops and tenderloins are easy to overcook. To keep them moist and tender, brush them thoroughly with an oil-based marinade. For extra flavor and moisture, top the cooked meat with a separate finishing sauce and let it stand for 5 minutes before serving.

Billiard Room Pizza Wheel

servings 8 to 10 **prep time** 10 minutes
baking time 35 minutes

1 package (16-ounce) fresh sage sausage, *Jimmy Dean®*
1 can (15½-ounce) black beans, rinsed and drained, *Goya®*
8 ounces roasted garlic tomato sauce, *Hunt's®*
2 tablespoons Mexican rice seasoning, *Lawry's®*
½ cup diced green bell pepper
½ cup diced red bell pepper
    All-purpose flour, for dusting
1 can (13.8-ounce) refrigerated pizza dough, *Pillsbury®*
1 cup shredded cheddar/Jack cheese blend, *Sargento®*
1 can (2.25-ounce) sliced ripe olives, drained, *Early California®*

1. Preheat oven to 375 degrees F.

2. In a large skillet, brown sausage over medium heat, breaking meat apart with a spoon. Drain sausage and discard fat. Add beans, tomato sauce, and Mexican rice seasoning. Cook over medium heat for 5 minutes, stirring occasionally. Add peppers; simmer for 8 minutes more. Set aside.

3. On a flour-dusted surface, roll dough to fit into a 15-inch round pizza pan. Spoon sausage filling around edge of dough. Top with cheese and olives. Using a pie cutter, begin from the center of the dough making 8 cuts; each will end at the start of the filling. This will create 8 triangles. Gently lift each triangle over the filling and tuck the tip under the edge of the dough.

4. Bake for 20 to 25 minutes or until crust is golden brown.

Crab Ravioli in Creamy Tomato Sauce

servings 8 **prep time** 30 minutes
cooking time 11 minutes

In the coastal regions of Italy, crabs are an integral part of the culture and crab ravioli is naturally a regional favorite. But cracking crabs and rolling out the pasta is a lot of work. My version simplifies the recipe by calling for canned crabmeat stuffed in wonton wrappers. Smothered in ricotta cheese and a creamy tomato sauce, this jewel of the sea is a delicacy for diners no matter where they may be.

1   can (6-ounce) lump crabmeat, drained, *Bumble Bee*®
½   cup ricotta cheese
1   teaspoon Italian seasoning, *McCormick*®
1   package (12-ounce) wonton wrappers, *Dynasty*®
1   egg, beaten
    All-purpose flour, for dusting
1   cup milk
1   package (1.3-ounce) creamy tomato sauce mix, *Knorr*®
2   tablespoons butter
    Chopped parsley, for garnish

1. Drain crabmeat, reserving liquid. For filling, in a small bowl, combine drained crabmeat, cheese, and Italian seasoning. Brush a wonton wrapper with the beaten egg. Place about ½ teaspoon crab filling in the center, and fold wrapper diagonally to form a triangle. Press edges to seal. Transfer to a flour-dusted baking sheet. Repeat until all crab filling has been used. (It should make about 32 ravioli.)

2. Bring a large pot of salted water to boil. Meanwhile, in a large saucepan over medium-high heat, combine milk and reserved crab liquid. Whisk in sauce mix. Add butter and bring to boil. Reduce heat and simmer, stirring frequently, for 3 minutes. Keep sauce warm over low heat while you boil the ravioli.

3. In batches of 8, drop ravioli into boiling water. Cook for 2 minutes or until ravioli rise to the surface. With a slotted spoon, carefully transfer ravioli to pan with sauce. Divide ravioli equally among 8 plates. Sprinkle with parsley and serve.

Angel Hair with Roasted Red Peppers, Feta, and Herb Dressing

servings 8
prep time 15 minutes

¹/₂	cup extra virgin olive oil, *Bertolli*®
¹/₃	cup finely chopped fresh herbs (basil, oregano, thyme)
2	tablespoons lemon juice, *ReaLemon*®
2	tablespoons water
¹/₂	teaspoon salt
	Freshly ground black pepper
1	package (16-ounce) angel hair pasta or spaghettini package, *Mancini*®
1	jar (12-ounce) roasted red peppers, *Mancini*®
¹/₄	red onion, slivered and soaked in cold water
4	ounces crumbled feta cheese, *Athenos*®
1	can (2¹/₂-ounces) sliced ripe olives, *Early California*®

1. For dressing, place oil, herbs, lemon juice, water, salt, and black pepper in a jar. Close lid tightly and shake until blended. Set aside.

2. Cook pasta according to package directions. Drain and place pasta in a large bowl. Add dressing to warm pasta and toss to combine. Add remaining ingredients. Toss gently to combine. Serve at room temperature.

Lemon Mascarpone Panna Cotta

servings 6 **prep time** 10 minutes
chilling time up to 48 hours

A hearty meal calls for a light, delicate dessert. Make this airy custard ahead of time for convenience and refrigerate it until you're ready to serve. For an elegant tone-on-tone presentation, arrange on a white plate and garnish with lemon zest or sugared lemon peel.

¹/₂ **cup boiling water**
1 **package (3-ounce) lemon gelatin,** *Jell-O*®
 Grated peel of 1 lemon
1 **cup mascarpone cheese**
1 **cup milk**
 Strips of lemon peel or fresh strawberries, raspberries, or other fruit of choice, for garnish

1. In a small bowl, combine water and lemon gelatin. Stir to dissolve gelatin completely. Stir in lemon peel.

2. In a medium saucepan, blend cheese and milk. Cook and stir over medium heat for 1 minute. Slowly stir in gelatin mixture to blend completely. Pour into six 6-ounce ramekins. Chill until set, then place plastic wrap directly on surface of each dessert.

3. Chill up to 48 hours. Garnish with lemon peel strips or fresh berries.

Tip: To make your own sugared lemon peel, wash a fresh lemon and dry thoroughly with paper towels. Cut the lemon into slices. Remove the rind and use a zester to curl it. Using a pastry brush, coat the top of the rind with pasteurized egg whites and sprinkle with superfine sugar. Let stand until dry.

Chocolate Hazelnut Torte

servings 10 to 12 **prep time** 10 minutes
baking time 20 minutes

2 tablespoons unsalted butter, softened
2 cups chopped hazelnuts
5 eggs
3 packages (3.9-ounce each) chocolate fudge instant pudding and pie filling mix, *Jell-O*®
½ cup butter, melted and cooled slightly
Cocoa powder and powdered sugar, for dusting

1. Preheat the oven to 325 degrees F.

2. Coat bottom and bottom inch of sides of a 10-inch springform pan with softened butter. Spread 1 cup chopped hazelnuts on bottom of pan.

3. In food processor or blender, combine remaining 1 cup hazelnuts, the eggs, pudding mixes, and melted butter. Process or blend until well mixed and nuts are ground. Pour into prepared pan.

4. Bake about 20 minutes or until edges of torte are firm but center jiggles when pan is shaken. Cool on a rack for 10 minutes. Release pan sides. Cool to lukewarm, then transfer to serving plate and dust with cocoa powder and powdered sugar. Serve warm or at room temperature.

Convert an old jelly jar into a shaker that's pretty enough to set on your counter. Simply fill the jelly jar with the cocoa-powdered sugar mixture and replace the canning lid with a heavy piece of lace. Place the screw band over top of lace and twist to secure.

Scropino

servings 2
prep time 3 minutes

2 scoops lemon gelato or sorbet
3 ounces citrus vodka, *Absolut®*
3 ounces lemoncello (lemon liqueur)
Italian Prosecco or sparkling white wine
Lemon slices, for garnish

1. In a blender, combine gelato, vodka, and lemoncello. Blend until smooth.

2. Divide between 2 glasses, then add Prosecco to fill glasses. Garnish with lemon slices.

Capri Fizzy

servings 1
prep time 3 minutes

4 large ice cubes
¼ cup *Campari®* liqueur
¼ cup strawberry nectar, *Kern's®*
Club soda, *Schweppe's®*
1 strip orange peel, for garnish

1. Place ice cubes in a tall glass. Pour Campari and strawberry nectar over ice. Add club soda to fill the glass. Twist the orange peel and drop into drink.

Mexican

In Mexico every meal is a cause for celebration, whether it's an ordinary weekday or Cinco de Mayo. The country is a cook's—and a diner's—paradise, a colorful cocktail of texture and flavor that's meant to be enjoyed on Mexico time; if not today, then mañana.

I could eat Mexican food morning, noon, and night. That's why this is a 24/7 chapter, a culinary trip to Margaritaville, where food and fiesta go hand in hand no matter when you serve it. Sweet or spicy, salty or tangy, every dish captures the bold, earthy flavors and laid-back charm that make Mexico so magical. Whether you choose chalupas and nachos or hot salsas and cool guacamole, it's high-spirited food for any occasion, from feeding the family to perking up a party. Serve on hand-painted crockery and pair with tart tequila-laced margaritas for festive flair on both sides of the border.

The Recipes

Guacamole

servings 8
prep time 10 minutes

2   large Hass avocados
2   tablespoons medium salsa, *Pace®*
1   tablespoon sour cream
1   tablespoon jalapeño juice (from jarred jalapeños)
    Salt

1. Peel avocados and remove pit. Place in a bowl and mash. Stir in salsa, sour cream, and jalapeño juice. Add salt to taste.

Serving Idea: Serve with Spicy Corn Chips (below).

Mesquite Salsa

servings 8
prep time 5 minutes

1   jar (24-ounce) chunky salsa, *Pace®*
1/3 cup chopped fresh cilantro
3   green onions, chopped
2   teaspoons mesquite marinade mix, *McCormick® Grill Mates®*

1. In a medium bowl, combine salsa, cilantro, green onions, and marinade mix.

Serving Idea: Serve with Spicy Corn Chips (below).

Spicy Corn Chips

servings 8 **prep time** 3 minutes per batch
baking time 5 minutes per batch

1   bag (1 pound 12 ounces) restaurant-style tortilla chips, *Mission®*
    Nonstick cooking spray, *PAM®*
1   packet (1.25-ounce) Tex-Mex chili seasoning, *McCormick®*

1. Preheat oven to 350 degrees F.

2. Working in batches, spread a single layer of chips on a baking sheet. Very lightly coat with nonstick spray. Lightly sprinkle with chili seasoning. Bake for 5 minutes. Repeat until all chips are seasoned.

Tortilla Soup with Grilled Chicken

servings 4 to 6 **prep time** 10 minutes
cooking time 15 minutes

2 **tablespoons corn oil**
1 **cup frozen diced onions,** *Ore-Ida®*
1 **carton (32-ounce) chicken broth,** *Swanson®*
1 **can (14.5-ounce) diced tomatoes with roasted garlic,** *Contadina®*
1 **can (4-ounce) diced green chiles, drained,** *Ortega®*
¼ **cup lime juice,** *RealLemon®*
2 **cups shredded grilled chicken breast**
   Salt and pepper
2 **cups broken tortilla chips**
   Chopped avocado, cilantro, and green onions

1. In a large saucepan, heat oil over medium-high heat. Add onions and cook for 3 minutes, stirring occasionally. Add broth, tomatoes, chiles, and lime juice. Bring to boil, then reduce heat and simmer 5 minutes. Stir in chicken and cook until just heated through, about 2 minutes. Season to taste with salt and pepper.

2. Ladle soup into bowls. Top each with tortilla chips. Serve with avocado, cilantro, and green onions.

V8® Gazpacho

servings 4 **prep time** 10 minutes
chilling time 1 hour

1 **bottle (32-ounce) vegetable juice,** *V8®*
1 **can (14.5-ounce) diced tomatoes with roasted garlic,** *Contadina®*
1 **small cucumber, seeded and diced**
1 **cup diced peeled jicama**
½ **cup chopped celery**
1 **can (4-ounce) diced green chiles,** *Ortega®*
   Salt and pepper
   Chopped avocado, chopped green onions, croutons, sour cream

1. In a large bowl, combine vegetable juice, tomatoes, cucumber, jicama, celery, and chiles. Cover and chill at least 1 hour or overnight. Season to taste with salt and pepper.

2. Ladle gazpacho into chilled bowls. Serve with avocado, green onions, croutons, and sour cream.

Shrimp and Jicama Ceviche

servings 4 **prep time** 10 minutes
chilling time 4 hours

- **8** **ounces fresh shrimp, peeled and deveined**
- **1** **avocado, peeled, pitted, and cut into chunks**
- **1** **cup diced peeled jicama**
- **3/4** **cup thick and chunky salsa, *Ortega*®**
- **1/4** **cup freshly squeezed lime juice**
- **Cilantro sprigs and lime wedges, for garnish**
- **Tortilla chips**

1. In a large bowl, combine shrimp, avocado, jicama, salsa, and lime juice. Chill for 4 to 6 hours, or until shrimp are opaque. Spoon equal amounts of shrimp mixture into 4 stemmed glasses or small bowls. Garnish with cilantro sprigs and lime wedges. Serve with tortilla chips.

Queso Fundido with Chile Rajas

servings 12 **prep time** 10 minutes
cooking time 5 minutes

- **1** **package (24-ounce) shredded Mexican cheese blend, *Kraft*®**
- **1** **can (7-ounce) whole green chiles, *Ortega*®**
- **1** **jar (12-ounce) roasted red peppers, *Mancini*®**
- **12** **green onions, sliced**
- **12** **corn tortillas, *Mission*®**

1. Preheat broiler. Place cheese in large shallow, oiled earthenware casserole or cast iron skillet. Slice chiles and peppers lengthwise. Sprinkle over cheese. Place under broiler just until cheese begins to melt. Scatter onions over peppers and continue to broil just until onions begin to color and cheese begins to bubble.

2. To heat tortillas, wrap tortillas in wet paper towels and heat in microwave on medium-high (75% power) about 15 seconds. To serve, scoop melted cheese mixture into tortillas.

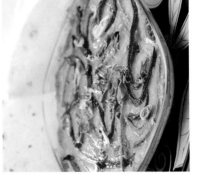

Grilled Fish in Corn Husks with Rice and Beans

servings 4 **prep time** 15 minutes
grilling time 10 minutes

In Mexico shucking and grinding corn for the afternoon meal is a daily ritual. This dish is the embodiment of *Semi-Homemade*®, delivering the same fresh flavor you would get from shucking and grinding your own corn without monopolizing your morning. The prepackaged corn husks keep the fish juicy and warm and fajita seasoning lends it authentic Mexican taste. Serve with Spanish rice and beans for a multi-cultural meal.

1	box (6.8-ounce) Spanish rice mix, *Rice-a-Roni®*
1	can (15.5-ounce) black beans, drained, *Goya®*
4	halibut or other firm white fish fillets (6 to 8 ounces each), 1 inch thick
2	tablespoons fresh lime juice
1	packet (1.25-ounce) Fajita seasoning mix, *Ortega®*
4	ears corn with husks
2	tablespoons butter, melted

1. Prepare rice according to package directions, adding beans during last 5 minutes of cooking time.

2. Meanwhile, sprinkle fish with lime juice and all but 1 tablespoon fajita seasoning. Remove husks from corn and cut corn into 3- to 4-inch chunks. Wrap husks around fish, tying with kitchen string to secure. Brush corn with melted butter and sprinkle with remaining fajita seasoning.

3. Grill fish directly over medium heat for 5 minutes. Turn fish over and grill 5 minutes more. Grill corn alongside fish, turning frequently.

Tip: To lock in moisture, soak the corn husks in water for several hours before wrapping the fish. To grill corn without burning, remove the tip of the corn at the silk end of the ear. Soak the corn in water for one hour. Then, grill corn for 15 minutes, turning every 3 minutes.

Mexican Pizza

servings 4 **prep time** 15 minutes
baking time 20 minutes

This eat-anytime-favorite has been known to reduce stress and induce happy moods—think of it as pizza therapy. A prebaked pizza round topped with a mix of melted cheeses and spicy chorizo makes a fun-for-all appetizer, lunch, or in-front-of-the-TV snack. To round out a meal, simply open a bag of salad and wha-la, dinner! Serve on a whimsical plate to play up its personality.

1 package (16-ounce) beef chorizo sausage, casing removed
½ cup medium salsa, *Pace®*
4 fully-baked pizza crusts (8 inch), *Boboli®*
1 can (16-ounce) refried black beans, *Rosarito®*
1 package (8-ounce) shredded Mexican cheese blend, *Kraft®*
  Shredded lettuce
  Finely chopped tomatoes
  Crushed tortilla chips
  Ranch dressing

1. Preheat oven to 400 degrees F. Cover a baking sheet with foil.

2. In a large skillet over medium heat, brown chorizo. Stir in salsa and simmer for 5 minutes. Lay pizza crusts on prepared baking sheet. Spread beans over pizza crusts. Spread chorizo mixture over beans. Cover pizzas with cheese.

3. Bake for 10 to 12 minutes or until cheese is melted. Remove from oven and top with lettuce, tomatoes, and tortilla chips. Place ranch dressing in a zip-top plastic bag; snip a corner off bag and pipe dressing over pizzas. Serve hot.

Fish Tacos

servings 4 **prep time** 10 minutes
cooking time 17 minutes

It took me a long time to try fish tacos in Mexico because I was convinced I wouldn't be a fan. Fish and tacos didn't seem to go together, but how wrong I was! Zesty seasonings and a vibrant presentation give this bit of Baja its signature zing. Serve them on colorful food-quality pottery for genuine made-in-Mexico charm.

³/4 **cup sour cream**
1 **package (1.25-ounce) taco seasoning mix, Ortega®**
1 **package (18.1-ounce) frozen fried fish tenders, Gorton's ®**
8 **corn tortillas, Mission®**
Avocado Cream (see recipe below)
2 **cups shredded green cabbage**
¹/2 **red onion, chopped (optional)**

1. Combine sour cream and taco seasoning. Prepare fish tenders according to package directions. Wrap tortillas loosely in wet paper towels and heat in microwave on medium-high (75% power) for 1 minute.

2. For each taco, place several fish tenders in a tortilla. Top with sour cream mixture, Avocado Cream, cabbage, and, if desired, red onion.

Tip: Set up a taco bar with guacamole, sour cream, cabbage, red onions, and taco sauce. Invite pint-size chefs to help. It's a kid-friendly way to warm them up to seafood. Throw in a piñata and Mexican favors such as maracas and poppers to make it a fiesta!

Avocado Cream

makes ³/4 cup
prep time 5 minutes

¹/2 **cup store-bought guacamole**
¹/4 **cup heavy cream**
Salt and pepper

1. Push guacamole through a fine-mesh sieve into a small bowl. (This will make the guacamole very smooth.) Whisk in cream. Season to taste with salt and pepper. Serve with Fish Tacos.

Crab and Shrimp Tostadas

servings 4 **prep time** 15 minutes
cooking time 5 minutes

- **2** cups cooked bay shrimp
- **2** cups flake-style imitation crabmeat, *Louis Kemp*®
- **1/2** cup refrigerated prepared fresh salsa
  Juice of 1 lime
- **1** can (16-ounce) refried black beans, *Rosarito*®
- **1½** cups thick and chunky salsa, *Ortega*®
- **4** tostada shells, *Ortega*®
- **1** bag (6-ounce) desired salad mix, *Ready Pac*®
- **1** avocado, peeled, pitted, and thinly sliced

1. In a large bowl, combine shrimp, crabmeat, fresh salsa, and lime juice. Cover and chill. In a large skillet, combine beans and salsa. Cook over medium heat until just heated through.

2. Place 1 tostada shell on each plate. Spread equal amounts of bean mixture over each shell. Top with salad mix and shrimp mixture. Arrange avocado slices over top.

Chicken Mini-Empanadas

servings 6 **prep time** 20 minutes
baking time 15 minutes

- **1** package (11-ounce) pie dough mix, *Betty Crocker*®
- **1** can (9.75-ounce) white chicken meat, drained, *Swanson*®
- **1** cup thick and chunky salsa, *Ortega*®
- **1** can (3-ounce) sliced ripe olives, *Early California*®
- **1** cup shredded Mexican cheese blend, *Kraft*®
  All-purpose flour, for dusting

1. Prepare pie dough according to package directions for double crust pie. Wrap dough in plastic wrap and chill.

2. Preheat oven to 400 degrees F. In a medium saucepan, combine chicken, salsa, and olives. Bring to boil, then reduce heat and simmer for 5 minutes. Remove from heat and stir in cheese. Cool slightly.

3. On a flour-dusted surface, roll dough ⅛ inch thick. Using a 3-inch round cutter, cut out 18 circles, rerolling scraps as needed. Place about 1 tablespoon chicken mixture in center of each circle. Moisten edges with water. Fold circles in half and pinch to seal. Pierce tops with fork.

4. Place empanadas on baking sheet. Bake for 15 minutes or until golden. Serve hot.

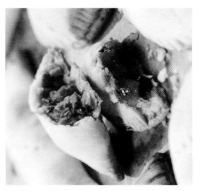

Green Corn Tamale Casserole

servings 6 to 8 **prep time** 15 minutes
baking time 45 minutes

2 ears corn with husks
1 stick butter
½ cup masa harina (tortilla flour), *Maseca*®
¼ cup evaporated milk, *Carnation*®
3 tablespoons yellow cornmeal, *Albers*®
½ teaspoon baking powder
1 can (7-ounce) chopped green chiles (undrained), *Ortega*®

1. Remove and reserve husks from corn. With the point of a sharp knife, cut through centers of corn kernels to release juices; reserve juices. Cut kernels from cobs. If desired, line an 8×8-inch glass baking pan or a 9-inch glass pie pan with corn husks, allowing husks to extend over rim of dish at least equal to the radius of the dish.

2. Preheat oven to 350 degrees F. In a food processor, combine butter and tortilla flour. Process until well blended. Add evaporated milk, corn-meal, and baking powder; process to mix. Add reserved corn juices, corn kernels, and green chiles. Process just to blend in corn. Transfer to prepared casserole. Fold husks over top of corn mixture.

3. Place an ovenproof plate or other weight on top of husks to hold in place. Bake 45 to 50 minutes or until firm. Cool slightly. To serve, cut into wedges or scoop out with spoon.

Tip: When cutting the corn off of the cob, place one end of the ear of corn on the tube of an angel food cake pan. The pan will catch the juice and keep the corn kernels from scattering.

Note: If corn on the cob is not in season, substitute 1 can (15-ounce) of low-sodium sweet corn, drained. Cover pan with aluminum foil when baking.

Las Chalupas

servings 4 to 6 **prep time** 15 minutes
cooking time 25 minutes

Meat
1   pound ground beef
1   package (1.25-ounce) taco seasoning mix, *Ortega*®
²/₃ **cup salsa, *Pace*®**
¹/₄ **cup jalapeño juice**

Tortillas
¹/₄ **cup canola oil, *Wesson*®**
4   to 6 flour tortillas (8 inch), *Mission*®

Toppings
Shredded Mexican cheese blend, *Kraft*®
Shredded lettuce
Chopped tomatoes
Chopped ripe olives
Store-bought guacamole
Sour cream

1. In a large skillet over medium heat, brown beef. Add taco seasoning, salsa, and jalapeño juice. Add a little water if mixture is too dry. Reduce heat to low and simmer for 10 minutes.

2. In another large skillet, heat oil over medium-high heat. Fry tortillas flat until crispy on both sides. Place tortillas on individual ovenproof plates. Cover each tortilla with meat mixture, then spread cheese over top.

3. Broil 6 inches from heat until cheese melts, about 2 minutes. Remove plates and top cheese with shredded lettuce, tomatoes, and olives. Place dollops of guacamole and sour cream in centers of chalupas.

Flan Cake

servings 6 to 8 **prep time** 15 minutes **cooking time** 25 minutes
baking time 35 minutes **cooling time** 10 minutes **chilling time** 2 hours

Flan is the Mexican version of crème caramel, a sweet custard baked in a water bath and flipped onto a plate for serving. I wasn't always a flan fan before *Semi-Homemade*, but this marvelously moist cake can win anyone over. It's unabashedly habit forming—not too dense and not too light, with a caramel glaze so rich it sends shivers down your spine. Serve it warm with coffee for dessert or cold with mango iced tea for a garden party, brunch or shower.

1   package (2.75-ounce) flan mix, *Jell-O*®
2   cups milk
2   egg yolks
1   box (9-ounce) yellow cake mix, *Jiffy*®
1   egg
½   cup water

1. Preheat oven to 350 degrees F.

2. Sprinkle contents of flan mix's caramel packet evenly over bottom of 8-inch round cake pan, spreading with back of spoon. Set aside.

3. In a medium saucepan, combine milk and flan mix. Stir over medium heat just until mixture comes to a boil. Place egg yolks in bowl and gradually whisk in hot milk mixture. Carefully pour over caramel in pan.

4. In a large bowl, combine cake mix, egg, and ¼ cup of the water. Stir to blend. Beat 300 strokes. Add remaining ¼ cup water and beat another 300 strokes. Spoon batter over flan mixture in pan. (Cake batter and flan will separate into layers as they bake.) Place pan in large roasting pan. Fill roasting pan with enough warm water to reach halfway up cake pan.

5. Bake 35 to 40 minutes. Cool for 10 minutes on wire rack, then refrigerate until chilled, at least 2 hours. Run a knife around edge of pan and invert onto serving plate, allowing caramel to drizzle over cake. Remove pan. Cut into wedges to serve.

Dulce de Leche Napoleons

servings 4 **prep time** 15 minutes
baking time 15 minutes

Vertical presentation is the height of restaurant fashion. This decadent recipe takes the classic **Napoleon** to a new level. **A tower of puff pastry layered with cool dulce de leche ice cream and served with a warm drizzle of caramel sauce gives new meaning to the words *melt in your mouth good.* Napoleons freeze beautifully, so bake them in batches and keep extra on hand for guests.**

   All-purpose flour, for dusting
1 **sheet frozen puff pastry, thawed, *Pepperidge Farm®***
1 **pint dulce de leche ice cream, softened slightly, *Breyers®***
1 **cup caramel sauce, *Mrs. Richardson's®***

1. Preheat oven to 400 degrees F.

2. On a flour-dusted surface, unfold pastry sheet. Cut pastry into 3 strips along fold marks. Cut each strip crosswise into 4 rectangles. Place the rectangles 2 inches apart on baking sheet. Bake about 15 minutes or until golden. Transfer to wire rack and cool.

3. Spread ice cream equally over 8 rectangles. Stack rectangles 2-high, then top with remaining 4 single rectangles to make four 3-layer Napoleons. Place on tray or in shallow baking dish and freeze until ready to serve.

4. In a glass measuring cup, microwave caramel sauce on medium-high (75% power) for 1 minute or until very warm. Place 1 Napoleon on each dessert plate. Drizzle with warm caramel sauce.

Tip: Frozen puff pastry is a shortcut you'll use time and again. Simply thaw, cut it into any shape you desire, and bake on parchment paper. If you don't use the entire package, seal the remaining sheets of pastry in a zip-top plastic bag and freeze until you need it.

Rosé Sangría

servings 6 to 8
prep time 5 minutes

2 cups rosé wine
2 cups *Sprite*®
³/₄ cup light rum, *Bacardi*®
³/₄ cup brandy, *Christian Brothers*®
Ice cubes
Apple slices
Green and red grapes, halved
Lemon slices
Lime slices

1. Combine wine, Sprite® rum, and brandy in a clear glass pitcher filled halfway with ice cubes. Stir with a long wooden spoon.

2. Add a few slices of apple, halved grapes, and lemon and lime slices to pitcher. Stir once more. Pour sangría into tulip glasses.

Beach Paradise

servings 1
prep time 5 minutes

Ice cubes
1 part dark rum, *Myers's*®
1 part guava nectar, *Kern's*®
¹/₂ lime, juiced
¹/₂ orange, juiced
1 teaspoon sugar
Dash grenadine
Slice mango, for garnish
Maraschino cherry, for garnish

1. Fill a cocktail shaker with ice cubes, add remaining ingredients, except mango and cherry. Shake well. Pour into a highball glass and garnish with a mango slice and maraschino cherry.

Asian

Asian cuisine is the feng shui of the food world, a harmonious balance of textures, temperatures, and flavors. Spices mingle with subtle complexity, and meals are edible art. Although I've always been a huge fan of Asian cooking, I was intimidated to make it at home. I never dreamed it could be so easy or turn out so beautifully with such little effort. Stir-fried, deep-fried, or steamed, the secret is to start with prepackaged products that save hours of work, without sacrificing taste.

Influenced by both the east (China) and the west (India), this chapter serves a banquet of ancient intercontinental delights concocted with a contemporary twist. Wonton Soup and Crispy Orange Beef make take-out-in an everyday treat, while Wasabi Crab on Green Onion Pancakes team with lychee nut saketini to give parties good karma. Stylish presentation is a main ingredient, so play up the drama by serving food in colorful paper take-out containers arranged on a silk remnant fabric that doubles as a tablecloth.

The Recipes

Wonton Soup

servings 4 to 6 **prep time** 20 minutes
cooking time 40 minutes

Wontons
- **8 ounces ground chicken**
- **1 packet (0.9-ounce) dried onion soup mix, *Lipton*®**
- **2 tablespoons sesame oil, *Sun Luck*®**
- **2 tablespoons oyster sauce, *China Bowl*®**
- **1 tablespoon bottled minced garlic, *McCormick*®**
- **24 wonton wrappers, *Melissa's*®**

Soup
- **1 boneless, skinless chicken breast, sliced into ¼-inch strips**
- **1 tablespoon bottled minced garlic, *McCormick*®**
- **1 tablespoon vegetable oil**
- **4 cans (14-ounce) chicken broth, *Swanson*®**
- **⅔ cup thinly sliced Chinese barbecued pork (char siu pork)**
- **2 tablespoons light soy sauce, *Kikkoman*®**
- **1 tablespoon sesame oil, *Sun Luck*®**
- **½ bag (12-ounce) frozen vegetable stir-fry mix, *Birds Eye Foods*®**
- **1 jar (4-ounce) sliced water chestnuts, drained**
- **1 jar (4-ounce) bamboo shoots, drained**

1. For wontons, combine the first 5 ingredients in a large bowl; mix well. Place ½ teaspoon of mixture in the center of each wonton wrapper. Moisten the sides of wrapper with water, then fold diagonally in half to form a triangle. Moisten the edges of the triangle and bring both points of the triangle's base towards the center to form a wonton shape. Set aside.

2. For soup, in a large pot over medium heat, sauté the chicken and garlic in the vegetable oil until chicken is no longer pink. Add the chicken broth, barbecued pork, soy sauce, and sesame oil. Simmer for 15 minutes. Add the wontons, and simmer for 10 minutes more. Add the frozen vegetables, water chestnuts, and bamboo shoots, and simmer for another 10 minutes.

Edamame in Kung Pao Sauce

servings 6 **prep time** 5 minutes
cooking time 10 minutes

- **1 pound frozen shelled edamame (green soybeans)**
- **2 carrots, diced**
- **½ onion, chopped**
- **2 tablespoons canola oil, *Wesson*®**
- **½ cup kung pao sauce, *Dynasty*®**
- **2 tablespoons low-sodium soy sauce, *Kikkoman*®**
- **1 teaspoon red pepper flakes, *McCormick*®**

1. Bring a pot of salted water to boil. Add edamame and return to boil. Cook for 5 minutes. Drain in a colander and set aside.

2. In a large skillet over medium heat, sauté diced carrots and chopped onion in oil until tender but not soft.

3. In a medium bowl, combine kung pao sauce, soy sauce, and red pepper flakes. Add edamame, carrots, and onion. Toss to coat. Serve warm.

Steamed Pork Bao Buns

servings 12 **prep time** 20 minutes
cooking time 25 minutes

- ⅓ **cup finely chopped green onions**
- 1½ **tablespoons bottled minced garlic, *McCormick®***
- 2 **tablespoons minced ginger**
- 2 **tablespoons vegetable oil**
- 3 **tablespoons hoisin sauce, *Sun Luck®***
- 3 **tablespoons oyster sauce, *China Bowl®***
- 3 **cups finely chopped Chinese barbecued pork (char siu pork)**
- 1 **tablespoon cornstarch**
- 2 **tablespoons cold water**
   All-purpose flour, for dusting
- 2 **cans (11-ounces each) refrigerated breadstick dough, *Pillsbury®***
- 1 **head Napa cabbage**

1. In a skillet over medium heat, sauté green onions, garlic, and ginger in oil until onions are tender. Stir in hoisin sauce and oyster sauce; add barbecued pork while stirring. Reduce heat to low. In a small bowl, combine cornstarch with the cold water. Pour over pork mixture and stir until sauce thickens. Set filling aside.

2. On a flour-dusted surface, partially separate breadsticks, leaving 2 thick layers of dough. Roll each into a ball. Working with 1 ball at a time, roll each ball out to make a 3-inch circle. Place about 1 tablespoon of filling in center of each circle. Gather dough up and twist tightly to secure. Cover with kitchen towel.

3. Arrange cabbage leaves on the bottom of 2 large bamboo steamers. Place 6 pork buns in each steamer. Steam buns for 20 minutes. Serve warm.

Frisée Salad with French Beans and Spicy Peanut Dressing

servings 6
prep time 15 minutes

Salad

- 1 bag (16-ounce) frozen French-cut green beans
- 1 head frisée lettuce
- 1/2 cup roasted peanuts, for garnish

Dressing

- 1/2 bunch green onions, chopped into 1/4-inch slices
- 3 tablespoons bottled minced garlic, *McCormick®*
- 1 tablespoon sliced ginger, *KAME®*
- 1 jalapeño, seeded and chopped into 1/2-inch pieces
- 2 tablespoons sesame oil, *Sun Luck®*
- 1 can (8.5-ounce) cream of coconut, *Coco Lopez®*
- 1 jar (18-ounce) smooth peanut butter
- 1 to 2 cups warm water
- 1/2 cup chopped cilantro
- 1/2 jar (8.5-ounce) hoisin sauce, *Sun Luck®*
- 1/4 cup low-sodium soy sauce, *Kikkoman®*

1. Thaw green beans in a colander and pat dry to remove excess water. Clean frisée and cut into bite-size pieces; set aside.

2. In a food processor, combine the green onions, garlic, ginger, and jalapeño. Process until uniform. Add the oil and process briefly to form a paste.

3. Transfer paste to a large bowl. Whisk in cream of coconut. Add peanut butter and 1 cup warm water. Add the remaining water, 1 tablespoon or so at a time, if necessary to make dressing a smooth consistency. Whisk in cilantro, hoisin sauce, and soy sauce.

4. Add green beans and frisée to bowl with dressing; toss until nicely coated. Garnish with roasted peanuts.

Thai Ginger Mussels

servings 2 to 3 **prep time** 10 minutes
cooking time 25 minutes

Asian meals are not served in courses. Appetizers, soups, meats, and vegetables are presented and eaten together. This dish, a spicy mix of ginger and Thai flavorings, enlivens all it accompanies. The bolder flavors bring out the mussels' subtle sweetness. Mimic the mood with dramatic servers in colors like black and red.

1   **can (13.5-ounce) coconut milk, *A Taste of Thai*®**
½   **cup white wine**
2   **tablespoons Thai ginger marinade, *Lawry's*®**
2   **tablespoons brown sugar**
1   **tablespoon curry paste (red or green), *Thai Kitchen*®**
1   **tablespoon bottled minced garlic, *McCormick*®**
3   **tablespoons butter, *Land O Lakes*®**
1   **pound fresh or thawed frozen mussels* (rinsed, de-bearded, and drained)**
2   **tablespoons chopped green onion, for garnish**

1. For sauce, in a medium saucepan, combine coconut milk, wine, marinade, brown sugar, curry paste, and half the garlic. Bring to boil over medium heat. Reduce heat and simmer for 20 minutes until sauce thickens and is reduced by half. Remove sauce from heat; set aside.

2. In a large skillet over medium-high heat, melt butter. Add mussels and the remaining garlic. Add ½ cup of sauce to mussels. Let simmer until mussels start to open, about 3 to 5 minutes. Transfer to a shallow bowl and spoon remaining sauce over top. Garnish with green onion.

Note: If mussels are not available, substitute one 12-ounce bag of uncooked large-count shrimp, *Contessa*®.

Tip: When choosing fresh mussels, discard mussels with broken or open shells. If a shell opens before cooking, gently tap it. If it does not close, throw it away. Also discard any mussels that do not open after they are cooked.

Wasabi Crab and Green Onion Pancakes

makes 24 pieces **prep time** 15 minutes
chilling time 1 hour **cooking time** 5 minutes

Wasabi Crab

2   cans (6 ounces each) lump crabmeat, drained, *Geisha®*
¼   cup wasabi mayonnaise, *French's®*
1   teaspoon fresh lemon juice or *ReaLemon®*
1   teaspoon finely chopped fresh chives
½   teaspoon low-sodium soy sauce, *Kikkoman®*

Green Onion Pancakes

4   flour tortillas (burrito size)
1   egg, lightly beaten
2   tablespoons thinly sliced green onions
    Chopped chives or prepared wasabi, for garnish

1. For wasabi crab, in a medium bowl, combine crabmeat, wasabi mayonnaise, lemon juice, chives, and soy sauce. Cover and chill mixture for 1 hour.

2. For green onion pancakes, use a pastry brush to lightly coat 1 side of each tortilla with egg. Sprinkle coated side of 2 tortillas with equal amounts of green onions. Place remaining 2 tortillas, coated side down, on top of tortillas with green onions. Press firmly together.

3. With a 2-inch round cutter (or empty tomato paste can with top and bottom removed), carefully cut 12 rounds from each tortilla sandwich. Place rounds in a dry, nonstick skillet over medium heat. Toast pancakes until golden brown on each side. Remove to plate and set aside.

4. To serve, spoon a small amount of wasabi crab on top of each pancake. Garnish with chopped chives or a very small amount of prepared wasabi.

Lemon Chicken

servings 6 **prep time** 10 minutes
cooking time 7 minutes

Maybe it's the satisfying crunch of warm crispy-fried batter mixed with the cool tang of lemon or maybe it's the undertone of sweet-tart ginger or the moist, tender chicken breast steeped in buttermilk. Whatever the reason, lemon chicken is an anytime-of-day favorite, as popular with kids as it is with adults.

Chicken

1 **quart buttermilk**
1 **tablespoon lemon zest**
4 **boneless, skinless chicken breasts, cut into strips**
2 **cups all-purpose flour**
1 **cup cornstarch**
Canola oil, for frying, *Wesson*®

Sauce

1 **jar (11-ounce) lemon curd, *Robertson's*®**
¼ **cup chicken broth, *Swanson*®**
½ **teaspoon soy sauce, *Kikkoman*®**
¼ **teaspoon ground ginger, *McCormick*®**
Sliced green onions, for garnish

1. For chicken, in a medium bowl, combine buttermilk and lemon zest. Add chicken and set aside. Sift together flour and cornstarch into a shallow dish.

2. In a large skillet, heat ¼ to ½ inch of oil to 365 degrees F. Shake excess buttermilk from chicken strips and dredge in flour mixture. Fry chicken strips in hot oil until golden brown on 1 side, about 4 to 5 minutes. Turn and finish cooking, another 3 to 4 minutes. Drain on paper towels. Set aside and keep warm.

3. For sauce, in a small saucepan over low heat, melt lemon curd, stirring constantly. Add broth, soy sauce, and ginger; heat through. Spoon sauce over fried chicken strips. Sprinkle with green onions.

Teriyaki
Salmon Strips

servings 4 prep time 15 minutes
marinate time 10 minutes cooking time 5 minutes

1½ **cups teriyaki sauce, divided,** *Kikkoman*®
1 **cup water**
10 **ounces king salmon, cut into 1-ounce strips**
10 **bamboo skewers, soaked in water for 30 minutes**
2 **tablespoons canola oil,** *Wesson*®
2 **tablespoons sesame seeds, for garnish,** *McCormick*®
2 **tablespoons chopped green onion, for garnish**

1. For marinade, in a shallow glass dish, combine 1 cup of the teriyaki sauce and the water. Thread salmon strips on presoaked skewers. Place skewers in marinade, turning to coat. Marinate for 10 minutes.

2. In a grill pan or large nonstick skillet, heat oil over medium-high heat. Cook the skewers for 3 minutes on each side for medium, or 5 minutes on each side for well done.

3. Arrange the skewers in a starlike pattern on a serving plate. Drizzle remaining ½ cup teriyaki sauce over the skewers. Garnish with sesame seeds and chopped green onion.

Serving Idea: Serve skewers on a bed of steamed rice.

Shiitake Rice
with Green Onions

servings 4 prep time 5 minutes
soak time 20 minutes
cooking time 10 minutes

3 **cups water**
6 **dried shiitake mushrooms, stems removed**
2 **cans (14.5 ounces each) low-sodium chicken broth,** *Swanson*®
2 **bags (2-cup size) boil-in-bag rice,** *Uncle Ben's*®
2 **chopped green onions**
2 **teaspoons light soy sauce,** *Kikkoman*®

1. In a large saucepan, combine water and shiitakes; bring to boil. Remove from heat and let soak for 20 minutes. With a slotted spoon, remove shiitakes from water and set aside. Add broth to the shiitake water and bring to boil. Immerse bags of rice in broth; boil, uncovered, for 10 minutes.

2. While rice is boiling, slice shiitakes. When rice is done, carefully remove bags from pot. Cut open bags and pour rice into a medium bowl. Add sliced shiitakes, green onions, and soy sauce. Toss to combine.

Shrimp in Spicy Coconut Sauce

servings 4 **prep time** 5 minutes
cooking time 10 minutes

When you're looking in the market for an ode to the Orient, this is the dish to turn to. A harmonious blend of spicy hot and creamy sweet, it offers something both for the yin and the yang. The shrimp's innate elegance makes an artistic presentation. Serve them on skewers to make crowd-pleasing party food or simply nest them on a bed of rice for a fix-it-fast meal.

1   teaspoon bottled minced garlic, *McCormick*®
1   tablespoon canola oil, *Wesson*®
1   cup light coconut milk, *A Taste of Thai*®
1/4 cup low-sodium chicken broth, *Swanson*®
2   teaspoons low-sodium soy sauce, *Kikkoman*®
1/4 cup heavy cream
1   pound peeled and deveined medium shrimp, cooked
2   tablespoons fresh cilantro leaves, for garnish

1. In a large skillet over medium heat, saute garlic in oil until fragrant. Stir in coconut milk, broth, and soy sauce. Bring to boil; reduce heat and simmer for 5 minutes. Stir in cream and return to a simmer (do not boil). Add shrimp and heat through. Garnish with cilantro leaves.

Crispy Orange Beef

servings 4 **prep time** 10 minutes
cooking time about 20 minutes

Beef

1½ pounds flank steak, cut into 1-inch strips
Salt and pepper
½ cup all-purpose flour
Vegetable oil, for frying

Sauce

1 teaspoon bottled minced garlic, **McCormick**®
1 tablespoon canola oil, **Wesson**®
½ cup orange marmalade, **Smucker's**®
1 cup low-sodium beef broth, **Swanson**®
10 small dried Thai chiles
1 teaspoon low-sodium soy sauce, **Kikkoman**®
2 teaspoons cornstarch

1. For beef, season flank steak strips with salt and pepper, then toss with flour. Shake off excess flour.

2. In a large skillet, heat ¼ to ½ inch vegetable oil to 365 degrees F. Working in batches, fry flour-coated steak strips until golden brown, about 3 to 4 minutes. (Do not crowd pan.) Drain on paper towels. Set aside and keep warm.

3. For sauce, in a medium saucepan over medium heat, saute garlic in canola oil until fragrant. (Do not let garlic brown.) Add orange marmalade, ½ cup of beef broth, the chiles, and soy sauce. Bring to boil; reduce heat and simmer for 5 minutes. In a small bowl, stir cornstarch into remaining ½ cup beef broth. Stir cornstarch mixture into simmering sauce. Return to simmer for 3 to 4 minutes until sauce thickens. Pour sauce over beef and serve.

Serving Idea: Serve on a bed of frisée and crispy fried rice noodles. Garnish with strips of orange peel.

Almond Cookies

makes 30 cookies **prep time** 15 minutes
baking time 13 minutes

1 container (18-ounce) refrigerated sugar cookie dough, *Pillsbury®*
1 tablespoon almond extract, *McCormick®*
½ cup ground blanched almonds
30 whole blanched almonds

1. Preheat oven to 325 degrees F.

2. In a large mixing bowl, combine cookie dough, almond extract, and ground almonds; mix well. Shape the dough into ½-inch balls. Place the balls about 2 inches apart on an ungreased cookie sheet. Gently press 1 whole almond into the center of each ball. Bake about 13 minutes or until golden. Cool on a wire rack.

Almond Chai Ice Cream

makes 1 quart **prep time** 2 minutes
cooking time 2 minutes **chilling time** 1 hour

2 cups heavy cream
6 tablespoons instant vanilla chai latte, *Pacific Chai®*
1 can (14-ounce) sweetened condensed milk, *Carnation®*
⅓ cup slivered almonds, toasted

1. Place 1 cup of cream in a large microwave-safe bowl. Microwave on medium-high (75% power) for 2 to 3 minutes or until steaming. (Do not boil.) Add instant chai latte; stir until dissolved. Stir in remaining 1 cup cream and the sweetened condensed milk. Cover and chill mixture for 1 hour.

2. Pour ice cream base into ice cream maker and follow manufacturer's instructions for freezing. When ice cream is thick and almost frozen, add toasted almonds. Finish freezing.

Note: Chai is a traditional Indian drink made from a blend of tea, milk, and ground spices (usually cardamom, cinnamon, cloves, ginger, nutmeg, and pepper).

BBQ

Barbequing is one of our grand old American traditions, a throwback to the time when cowboys huddled around the campfire and grilled slabs of beef over fragrant embers. The smell was an invitation to relax, socialize, and enjoy life. It still is. During the week, we work hard, but when the weekend comes, we're ready to grill and chill. I'm a country girl at heart, yearning for that slow-cooked smoky taste no matter how tight the time.

Whether you're firing up the grill outside—or the microwave inside—these down-home delights are the best of carefree cooking, summer or winter. Babyback ribs are so tender they fall off the bone, the beer bratwurst and kraut celebrate Oktoberfest no matter what the season and the chili omelet is so tongue-tingling good, I've even airmailed its ingredients to friends in France for a quick fix. Served plain or fancy, with saucy sides, and kick-back cocktails, it's All-American soul food at its simplest.

The Recipes

Baked Beans

servings 6 to 8 **prep time** 8 minutes
cooking time 35 minutes

½   **pound slab bacon, chopped into ½-inch pieces**
2   **cans (32-ounce each) baked beans**
½   **cup ketchup, _Heinz®_**
⅓   **cup brown sugar, _C&H®_**
2   **tablespoons hot pepper sauce, _Tabasco®_**
2   **tablespoons honey, _Sue Bee®_**

1. In a heavy pot or Dutch oven, cook the bacon over medium heat just until the fat begins to render, about 4 minutes. Add beans, ketchup, brown sugar, hot pepper sauce, and honey. Bring to boil. Reduce heat and simmer for 25 to 30 minutes or until flavors are combined.

Sour Cream and Chive Biscuits

makes 8 **prep time** 10 minutes
baking time 8 minutes

2   **cups buttermilk baking mix, _Bisquick®_**
⅔   **cup sour cream**
2   **tablespoons finely chopped chives**
    All-purpose flour, for dusting
2   **tablespoons milk**

1. Preheat oven to 450 degrees F.

2. In a large mixing bowl, combine baking mix, sour cream, and chives until soft dough forms.

3. Turn dough onto a floured surface and knead 10 to 12 times. Roll dough to ½-inch thickness. With a 2½-inch round cutter or an empty drinking glass, cut 8 rounds from dough. Place rounds on an ungreased baking sheet and brush with milk.

4. Bake for 8 to 10 minutes or until golden brown. Serve warm with butter.

Canned Cornbread Muffins

makes 10 minutes
baking time 20 minutes

2 boxes (8.5 ounces each) corn muffin mix, *Jiffy®*
2 cups creamed corn, *Green Giant®*
1½ cups shredded Jack and cheddar cheese blend, *Sargento®*
⅔ cup buttermilk
2 large eggs
10 empty cans (6-ounce) tomato paste, cleaned
   Butter-flavored nonstick cooking spray, *PAM®*

1. Preheat oven to 400 degrees F.

2. In a large bowl, combine muffin mix, creamed corn, 1 cup of cheese, the buttermilk, and eggs. Set aside.

3. Spray inside of empty cans with cooking spray. Fill each can about two-thirds full with muffin batter. Sprinkle remaining ½ cup shredded cheese evenly over top of batter. Place cans on baking sheet and bake for 20 minutes or until golden brown.

Cheesy BBQ Corn-on-the-Cob

servings 6 **prep time** 10 minutes
grilling time 15 minutes

6 ears corn
1 stick butter, softened
1 teaspoon chili powder, *McCormick®*
1 packet (1.3-ounce) creamy cheese sauce mix, *Knorr®*
   (or powdered cheese packet from boxed macaroni and cheese)

1. Preheat grill for medium direct heat or preheat oven to 350 degrees F.

2. Shuck ears of corn. (If desired, leave the husks attached to cobs to use as holders.)

3. In a small bowl, combine softened butter, chili powder, and cheese sauce mix. Spread butter mixture on corn and wrap each in foil.

4. Grill, covered, for 15 to 20 minutes, turning every 5 minutes. Or roast in preheated oven for 15 to 20 minutes (do not turn, if roasting).

Beer Brats and Kraut

servings 6 **prep time** 5 minutes
cooking time 10 minutes

3   **bottles (12 ounces each) dark beer**
6   **brats**
1   **jar (25-ounce) sauerkraut, *Bubbies*®**
6   **sesame brat buns or hot dog buns**
    Dijon mustard or yellow mustard, *French's*®

1. Pour beer into a large pot and heat over medium heat. Place brats and sauerkraut in beer. Simmer for 10 minutes. With tongs, remove brats from beer and place 1 in each bun. Using a slotted spoon, spoon sauerkraut over brats. Drizzle mustard on top.

Babyback Ribs

servings 4 **prep time** 5 minutes
cooking time 1 hour **grilling time** 8 minutes

Summertime (or wintertime), the grilling is easy when you cook this stick-to-your-ribs dish. The shortcut is to simmer the ribs in beef stock, cooking them most of the way, then baste them with sauce while they sizzle on the grill. Serve with Baked Beans (page 96), Canned Cornbread Muffins (page 99), and Lime Beer Cocktails (page 116) for a dinner that's downright delicious any time of year.

2   **full racks babyback ribs, quartered**

4   **cups beef broth, *Swanson*®**
    Water

2   **cups barbecue sauce, *Bullseye*® *Original***

1   **cup honey, *Sue Bee*®**

1. Place ribs and broth in a large heavy pot or Dutch oven. Add enough water to cover ribs. Bring to boil. Reduce heat and simmer about 1 hour or until tender. Remove ribs from pot; set aside.

2. Preheat grill for medium-direct heat. In a medium bowl, combine barbecue sauce and honey. Baste ribs generously with sauce. Grill ribs, uncovered, for about 4 minutes per side or until desired doneness.

Grilled Beer Salmon

servings 4 to 6 **prep time** 10 minutes
grilling time 8 minutes

Almost anything tastes better cooked on the grill, especially salmon. This is my sister Kimber's salmon supper, which always makes a splash. The secret is in her sauce—a buttery blend of sweet brown sugar, salty garlic, and full-bodied beer. Everyone in the family loves it. For stronger flavor, use a dark beer or ale; for more subtle flair, use a lighter beer.

1   1½-pound salmon fillet (12-inch tail piece)
2   teaspoons garlic salt, *McCormick*®
3   tablespoons brown sugar, *C&H*®
4   tablespoons butter, cut into small pieces
1   small red onion, thinly sliced
1   bottle (12-ounce) beer

1. Preheat grill for medium-high direct heat.

2. Using aluminum foil, create an oblong cooking tray, approximately 13×8×2-inches. (Make sure tray is watertight.) Place salmon fillet in center of tray. Season with garlic salt, then sprinkle with brown sugar. Dot with pieces of butter and top with onion slices.

3. Place tray on grill. Pour beer into tray to just below the highest point of fillet. Cover tray with aluminum foil to envelop fish completely. Cover grill with lid. Grill about 8 minutes or until salmon just begins to flake.

Cowboy Tri-Tip

servings 4 **prep time** 25 minutes
grilling time 20 minutes **stand time** 10 minutes

Dry Rub
2 tablespoons chili powder, *McCormick®*
2 tablespoons ground cumin, *McCormick®*
1 tablespoon seasoned pepper (salt free), *Lawry's®*
1 tablespoon onion powder, *McCormick®*
1 tablespoon garlic powder, *McCormick®*

1 1½-pound tri-tip roast
  Kosher salt

BBQ Sauce
1 jar (26-ounce) pasta sauce, *Prego® Traditional*
1 tablespoon chili powder, *McCormick®*
2 teaspoons dry mustard, *McCormick®*
2 tablespoons Worcestershire sauce, *Lea & Perrins®*
1 tablespoon honey, *Sue Bee®*

1. Preheat grill for medium-direct heat.

2. For dry rub, in a small bowl combine all dry rub ingredients. Set aside.

3. Rinse roast with cold water and pat completely dry with paper towels. Place roast on plate or platter and season with kosher salt. Rub a generous amount of dry rub into both sides of meat. Let rest for 10 to 15 minutes. Repeat rub and rest 2 to 3 times until all seasoning is used.

4. While meat is resting between rubs, prepare BBQ sauce. In a saucepan over medium heat, combine all sauce ingredients. Bring to boil. Reduce heat and simmer for 15 minutes. Set aside.

5. Grill roast about 20 minutes for medium-rare, turning and mopping with sauce every 5 minutes. Transfer roast to cutting board. Tent with foil; let stand 10 minutes. Cut roast diagonally across grain. Serve with extra sauce.

BBQ Chicken Pizza

servings 4 to 6 **prep time** 15 minutes
cooking time 12 minutes **baking time** 20 minutes

2 tablespoons olive oil, *Bertolli®*
½ pound chicken tenders
⅔ cup barbecue sauce, *Bullseye® Original*
All-purpose flour, for dusting
1 package (13.8-ounce) refrigerated pizza dough, *Pillsbury®*
1 cup shredded mozzarella cheese
¾ cup shredded Gouda cheese
¾ cup shredded Parmesan cheese, *Kraft®*
½ medium red onion, thinly sliced
3 tablespoons chopped fresh cilantro leaves

1. Preheat oven to 400 degrees F.

2. In a large skillet over medium-high heat, heat oil. Add the chicken tenders and saute until golden brown, about 12 minutes. Remove from heat. When chicken is cool enough to handle, chop chicken. In a small bowl, toss chicken with 2 tablespoons of barbecue sauce. Set aside.

3. On a flour-dusted surface, roll out pizza dough to fit a greased 15×10×1-inch sheet pan; place on pan. Shape dough to fill pan. Spread remaining barbecue sauce evenly over pizza dough. Sprinkle cheeses, onion, and chicken over sauce.

4. Bake about 20 minutes or until cheese bubbles. Sprinkle with chopped cilantro.

Outback Chili Omelet

servings 3 **prep time** 10 minutes
cooking time 5 minutes + 8 minutes per omelet

You can describe this all-day dish as home on the range meets diner food. It's a bountiful blue plate special that hits the spot for breakfast, brunch, or dinner. Three eggs and three cheeses lay the foundation for canned chili doctored up with spicy sausage and topped with a dollop of sour cream and chives. The result is a clean-your-plate meal in short order.

1 package (6-ounce) sausage patties, *Jimmy Dean*®
3 tablespoons butter
9 eggs
¼ cup chopped fresh chives
1 can (15-ounce) chili with beans, *Hormel*®
1 package (8-ounce) shredded Mexican cheese blend, *Sargento*®
    Sour cream

1. Crumble sausage into a medium skillet. Brown sausage over medium heat, stirring frequently to break up clumps. Drain and set aside.

2. In a medium skillet over medium-low heat, melt butter. Whisk together 3 of the eggs and 1 tablespoon of the chives. Pour egg mixture into skillet and cook without stirring just until eggs are firm, lifting edges to let uncooked egg run underneath.

3. Cover half of the cooked eggs with ¼ cup of the chili, ⅓ cup of the browned sausage, and ¼ cup of the cheese. Fold omelet and slide from skillet onto a plate.

4. Top omelet with another ¼ cup each of the cheese and chili. Add a dollop of sour cream and sprinkle with 1 teaspoon of chives. Repeat steps 2 through 3 with the remaining ingredients to make two more omelets.

*Note: Omelets can be prepared up through step 3 and held, covered, in a 200 degree F oven until all the omelets have been prepared.

Chocolate
Buttermilk Pie

servings 8 to 10 **prep time** 15 minutes
baking time 1 hour 15 minutes

I first tasted this deep-dish delight at Bubba's Barbeque in Jackson Hole, Wyoming, where locals and tourists alike wait in line for a slice of this little piece of heaven. It was so amazing, I went back in the kitchen and watched them make it, then brought the recipe home. A silky blend of chocolate and vanilla paired with a punch of buttermilk, this old-fashioned favorite is about as homegrown as it gets. If you want to go all out, top each piece with a fluffy cloud of whipped cream dusted with cocoa.

1½ **cups semisweet chocolate morsels,** *Nestle*®
1½ **cups sugar,** *C&H*®
¼ **cup all-purpose flour**
½ **teaspoon salt**
6 **eggs**
1 **cup buttermilk**
1½ **tablespoons vanilla extract,** *McCormick*®
1 **premade deep-dish piecrust (9-inch)**
    Frozen whipped topping, thawed, *Cool Whip*®

1. Preheat oven to 325 degrees F. Position a rack in center of oven.

2. Place the chocolate chips in a double boiler; melt over low heat, stirring constantly.

3. In a medium bowl, whisk together sugar, flour, and salt. In a large mixing bowl, combine the eggs, buttermilk, and vanilla. Add the sugar mixture and beat with an electric mixer or whisk vigorously until well combined. Stir the melted chocolate into the batter.

4. Pour batter into piecrust. (You will have about 1 cup of batter left over.) If desired, pour leftover batter into a 10- to 12-ounce buttered ramekin, custard cup, or other small baking dish.

5. Bake pie for 1 hour and 15 minutes to 1 hour and 25 minutes (and ramekin of leftover batter for 40 to 50 minutes) or until the pie is crisp on top and a knife inserted in the center comes out with just a bit of moist chocolate on it.

6. Remove pie from oven and cool on a cooling rack. If not eating immediately, refrigerate pie. Let refrigerated pie stand at least 1 hour at room temperature before serving. Garnish with whipped topping just before serving.

Tip: For a from scratch whipped topping flavor, simply doctor Cool Whip® with vanilla extract.

Cherry Lattice Pie

servings 8 prep time 15 minutes
baking time 40 minutes **stand time** 20 minutes

- 1 can (21-ounce) cherry pie filling or topping, *Comstock More Fruit®*
- 12 ounces frozen mixed berries, thawed and drained
- 1 tablespoon Kirsch (cherry brandy)
- 1 package (15-ounce) refrigerated piecrust, *Pillsbury®*
  All-purpose flour, for dusting
- 1 egg, lightly beaten
- 1 tablespoon sugar, *C&H®*

1. Preheat oven to 375 degrees F. In a large bowl, combine cherry pie filling, mixed berries, and Kirsch. Set aside.

2. Gently press 1 sheet of piecrust into flour-dusted pie plate. Pour berry filling into unbaked crust. Using a pie plate as a guide, cut a circle for the top crust from second sheet of piecrust. Use a generously floured lattice cutter to cut a pattern from circle. Top pie with lattice strips. Press along rim to seal and trim edges. Press fork into edges or crimp to make decorative edge. Brush top crust with beaten egg and sprinkle lightly with sugar.

3. Bake for 40 minutes or until filling bubbles. Cover pie with foil halfway through baking to prevent overbrowning. Let stand for 20 minutes before serving.

Double Strawberry Pie

servings 8 prep time 20 minutes
baking time 1hour

- 4 cups frozen unsweetened strawberries, partially thawed in refrigerator
- ³/₄ cup sugar, *C&H®*
- 4 tablespoons cornstarch
- 1 box (11-ounce) piecrust mix, *Betty Crocker®*
- ¹/₃ cup strawberry nectar, chilled, *Kern's®*
  All-purpose flour, for dusting
- 1 egg, beaten with 1 tablespoon water
  Sugar, *C&H®*

1. Preheat oven and a baking sheet to 450 degrees F. Place strawberries in a large bowl. Sift the ³/₄ cup sugar and the cornstarch over the partially thawed strawberries. Stir to combine; set filling aside.

2. In a medium bowl, combine crust mix and strawberry nectar. Stir until soft dough forms. Divide into 2 pieces, form balls, and flatten into disks. On a flour-dusted surface, roll 1 of the disks 1½ inches larger than an inverted 9-inch pie plate. Fold rolled dough in half, place in pie plate, and unfold. Press dough into plate but do not stretch. Trim dough ½ inch from edge of plate.

3. Roll out second disk and fold in half. Pour filling into bottom crust. Place top crust over filling and unfold. Press along rim to seal and trim edges. Press fork into edges or crimp to make decorative edge. Cut vent slits in top crust or punch center with small decorative cutter. Brush crust with beaten egg mixture. Sprinkle with sugar.

4. Place pie on preheated baking sheet in oven. Bake for 10 minutes. Reduce heat to 350 degrees F; continue baking for 50 to 60 minutes or until filling is bubbly and crust is golden brown. Cool completely before cutting.

White Wine Cooler

servings 6 **prep time** 5 minutes
chill time 1 hour

1   bottle (750 ml) white wine, chilled, such as Riesling
1   can (15-ounce) sliced peaches in heavy syrup, *Del Monte*®
½   cup orange-flavored liqueur, *Cointreau*®
½   cup orange juice
¼   cup sugar, *C&H*®
1   orange, sliced

1. In a large pitcher, combine wine, peaches with syrup, liqueur, orange juice, and sugar; stir well. Add orange slices to pitcher. Cover tightly and refrigerate for 1 hour. Pour into 6 wine glasses and serve immediately.

Lime Beer Cocktail

servings 6
prep time 5 minutes

6   bottles (12 ounces each) light beer
1   can (12-ounce) frozen limeade concentrate, *Minute Maid*®
1   lime, cut in half

1. Pour beer into a large pitcher. Add frozen limeade; stir to combine. (Stirring with a metal utensil reduces foam.) Allow foam to settle. Squeeze one lime half into pitcher. Thinly slice the other lime half; add slices to pitcher, for garnish. Pour into chilled glasses and serve cold.

From left to right:
Lime Beer Cocktail
and White Wine Cooler

Comfort Food

By whatever name you call it—retro food, diner food, feel-good food—comfort food is a culinary hug, the tried-and-true favorites that make everybody feel loved. In a stressful world, it's comforting to revisit a time when Mom's meatloaf or just-baked cookies created a feeling of warmth and safety.

I'm a comfort food fan, whether I'm indulging myself or others. This chapter offers a soul-soothing stroll down memory lane by way of the kitchen. Each dish is a time-tested throwback with a Zen spin—chewy chocolate brownies with mounds of mocha icing, creamy clam chowder served in a crusty bread bowl, macaroni and cheese made with American, Italian, or Mexican flavorings. The point of serving comfort food is comfort itself, so keep it cozy. Gather your friends and eat in the kitchen, on the deck, or in front of TV trays in the den.

The Recipes

Sandra and her dog Aspen.

Chicken and Dumplings

servings 8 **prep time** 15 minutes
cooking time 50 minutes

2 whole (2-pound) store-bought deli roasted chickens
2 tablespoons vegetable oil
1 package (7-ounce) chopped onions, *Ready Pac*®
1 container (14-ounce) carrot sticks, chopped, *Ready Pac*®
1 container (14-ounce) celery sticks, chopped, *Ready Pac*®
6 cans (14 ounces each) low-sodium chicken broth, *Swanson*®
2 teaspoons poultry seasoning, *McCormick*®
1 teaspoon salt
½ teaspoon black pepper
 All-purpose flour, for dusting
1 container (16.3-ounce) refrigerated buttermilk biscuit dough, *Pillsbury® Grands!*®
1 can (10.5-ounce) condensed chicken gravy, *Campbell's*®

1. Remove skin and bones from chickens; shred meat into large pieces. Set aside.

2. In a large heavy pot or Dutch oven, heat oil over medium heat. Add onions, carrots, and celery. Cook until soft, about 10 minutes.

3. Add broth, poultry seasoning, salt, pepper, and chicken. Bring to boil. Reduce heat and simmer for 30 minutes.

4. While stew simmers, prepare dumplings. On a flour-dusted surface, roll each biscuit ¼ inch thick. With a pizza cutter, cut biscuits into 1-inch-wide strips. Set aside.

5. Skim off any scum that has risen to surface of soup. Stir in chicken gravy. Stir in dumplings, a few at a time. Cover with a tight-fitting lid and simmer for 10 minutes more. Ladle into bowls and serve piping hot.

Grilled Cheese
Dippers with Spicy
Tomato-Cheese Soup

servings 4 **prep time** 10 minutes
cooking time 10 minutes

Grilled Cheese Dippers
1 **can (10³/₄-ounce) condensed Southwest-style pepper Jack soup, *Campbell's*®**
8 **ounces shredded Mexican cheese blend, *Kraft*®**
1 **baguette French bread, sliced ¹/₂ inch thick**
¹/₂ **stick butter, softened**

Spicy Tomato-Cheese Soup
1 **can (10³/₄-ounce) condensed tomato soup, *Campbell's*®**
1 **can (10³/₄-ounce) condensed cheddar cheese soup, *Campbell's*®**
3 **cups spicy vegetable juice, *V8*®**
2 **teaspoons hot pepper sauce, *Tabasco*®**
1 **teaspoon dried basil, *McCormick*®**

1. For grilled cheese dippers, in a bowl, combine pepper Jack soup and the shredded cheese. Spread mixture on half of the baguette slices; top with the remaining baguette slices. Butter the outside of the sandwiches.

2. Heat large skillet or griddle over medium-high heat. Place sandwiches in the skillet and cook until golden brown, approximately 2 minutes per side. Cover skillet to ensure the cheese melts.

3. For spicy tomato-cheese soup, combine all soup ingredients in a medium saucepan. Heat through over medium heat, stirring occasionally. Serve in mugs with Grilled Cheese Dippers.

Mini Burgers on Toasted Disks

makes 32 **prep time** 20 minutes
baking time 30 minutes

8 thin slices white bread
   Olive oil nonstick cooking spray, *PAM*®
1 pound lean ground beef
1 packet (1-ounce) pot roast seasoning, *Lawry's*®
1 egg, lightly beaten
2 tablespoons Worcestershire sauce, *Lea & Perrins*®
   Ketchup and/or mustard

1. Preheat oven to 400 degrees F.

2. Using a 1¾-inch round pastry cutter, cut 32 circles out of bread slices. Arrange disks on a baking sheet and spray lightly with cooking spray. Bake disks about 7 minutes or until toasted. Cool completely.

3. In a large bowl, combine beef, pot roast seasoning, egg, and Worcestershire sauce. Form 1-inch meatballs using 1 tablespoon of meat mixture per ball. Place meatballs 1 inch apart on a broiler pan. Using your index finger, gently poke holes in the middle of each meatball.

4. Bake for 12 minutes. Turn on broiler and broil for 5 minutes more. Remove from oven. Let stand on baking sheet for 7 minutes before transferring to toasted disks. Gently fill each burger hole with ketchup and/or mustard. Serve warm.

Poker Potato Chips

servings 6 to 8 **prep time** 15 minutes
chill time 20 minutes **cooking time** 15 minutes

1 cup all-purpose flour
4 packets (0.6-ounces each) roasted garlic dressing mix, *Good Seasons*®
2 medium sweet potatoes
2 large red skin potatoes
   Vegetable oil, for deep-frying
   Salt and pepper

1. In a large resealable plastic bag, combine flour and dressing mix; set aside.

2. Rinse potatoes and pat dry with paper towels. Using a mandoline slicer, thinly slice potatoes into round disks. Starting with sweet potatoes, add about half of the slices to the seasoned flour. Seal bag and shake. Arrange slices on a baking sheet; repeat with remaining potatoes. Chill seasoned potatoes about 20 minutes.

3. In a large, heavy-bottomed Dutch oven heat enough oil to rise a little less than halfway up the sides of the pot. Heat oil to 375 degrees F. Fry potato slices in small batches until crisp. Remove with slotted spoon and drain on paper towels. Season to taste with salt and pepper. Repeat with remaining potato slices.

Spaghetti with Garlic Meat Sauce

servings 4 to 6
prep time 10 minutes
cooking time 25 minutes

Anyone who samples this homey entrée will swear the recipe has been lovingly passed down for generations. Only you'll know it started with you—and a jar of Newman's Own® marinara sauce. A glass of robust red wine gives the sauce its rich flavor. The alcohol in the wine evaporates with cooking, making it a family-friendly choice for all occasions.

- 4 tablespoons olive oil, *Bertolli®*
- 4 tablespoons butter
- 2 tablespoons minced fresh garlic
- 1 package (8-ounce) sliced fresh mushrooms
- 1 jar (6.5-ounce) peeled garlic cloves, *Christopher Ranch®*
- 1½ pounds lean ground beef
- 1 jar (26-ounce) mushroom marinara sauce, *Newman's Own®*
- ⅔ cup red wine (Merlot or Cabernet)
- 2 tablespoons Italian seasoning, *McCormick®*
- 1 box (16-ounce) spaghetti
  Salt

1. In a large skillet over medium heat, heat olive oil and butter. When butter melts, add minced garlic and saute for 20 seconds. Add mushrooms and peeled garlic cloves; saute for 3 minutes. Add beef and cook until browned. Add marinara sauce, wine, and Italian seasoning. Stir to combine. Cover skillet. Reduce heat to low and simmer for 15 minutes to combine flavors.

2. Meanwhile, cook spaghetti in a large pot of boiling salted water until al dente, about 8 to 10 minutes. Drain. Toss hot pasta with the sauce.

Chicken-Fried Steak with Gravy

servings 4 **prep time** 10 minutes
cooking time 20 minutes

This pan-fried specialty started down south, in Texas, where it's affectionately called CFS. It's a budget-smart way to dress up inexpensive cubed steak by skillet frying it like chicken and smothering it in a sopping-good buttermilk gravy. Serve with a side of mashed potatoes for a Southern-style dinner, then top the leftovers with lettuce, tomato, and mayo for lunch the next day.

1 cup all-purpose flour
2 packets (1 ounces each) dry ranch dressing mix, *Hidden Valley®*
Salt and pepper
3 cups buttermilk
1 egg, lightly beaten
1 pound cubed steak, cut into 4 pieces
Oil, for frying
1 cup chicken broth, *Swanson®*
1 packet (2.64-ounce) country gravy mix, *McCormick®*
Mashed potatoes (optional)

1. In a large resealable plastic bag, combine flour, 1 packet dressing mix, and salt and pepper. Set aside. In a shallow bowl, combine 2 cups of the buttermilk, the remaining packet of dressing mix, and the egg.

2. Soak steaks in buttermilk mixture. Remove 1 steak, letting excess buttermilk mixture drip off. Add to flour mixture, seal bag, and toss to coat. Shake off any excess flour and dip again in the buttermilk mixture. Return to flour mixture, seal bag, and toss; set aside. Repeat process for remaining steaks.

3. In a large cast-iron skillet, heat 1/2 inch oil to 350 degrees F. Fry 2 steaks in the pan at a time for 4 minutes per side or until golden brown. Drain on paper towels. Set aside and keep warm.

4. For gravy, in a small saucepan, combine remaining 1 cup buttermilk, the broth, and gravy mix. Bring to a simmer over medium heat and stir well. Spoon gravy over steaks and, if desired, serve with mashed potatoes.

Tip: No matter how experienced you are, gravy making requires some trial-and-error effort. Cream gravy is meant to be thick, but if it gets doughy or lumpy, stir in small amounts of liquid until it reaches the consistency you want.

Mini Chicken Pot Pies

makes 12 appetizers **prep time** 15 minutes
cooking time 45 minutes

Who wouldn't take quick comfort in these petite pies stuffed with herbed vegetables and tender bites of white meat chicken? A scaled-down version of the kind Mom made, these minis feature frozen vegetables, canned chicken breast, and ready-made phyllo dough. Each pie is baked in an espresso cup—a cute contemporary twist that perks up any occasion.

⅓	cup chicken broth, *Swanson®*
8	ounces frozen mixed vegetables (corn, peas, carrots)
2	cans (10 ounces each) chicken breast, drained, *Hormel®*
½	can (10¾-ounce) condensed cream of celery soup, *Campbell's®*
1	tablespoon garlic herb seasoning blend, *McCormick®*
¼	cup butter, melted
5	sheets phyllo dough, *Athens Foods®*
	Black pepper

1. Preheat oven to 375 degrees F.

2. In a medium saucepan over medium heat, heat broth. Add frozen vegetables and chicken; simmer for 15 minutes. Add soup and seasoning blend; cook for another 5 minutes. Set aside.

3. Arrange 12 oven-safe espresso (demitasse) cups 2 inches apart on a baking sheet lined with parchment paper. Fill each cup with 1 heaping tablespoon chicken mixture.

4. Brush melted butter over each sheet of phyllo dough, and cut each sheet into 3-inch squares. Top each cup with 5 phyllo squares; fold ends toward sides of cups.

5. Bake pot pies for 25 minutes or until phyllo turns golden brown and sheets puff up. Serve warm.

To reheat: Place chilled cups on a baking sheet; loosely cover with parchment paper or foil. Bake at 300 degrees F for 10 minutes.

Mexican-Style Macaroni and Cheese

servings 4 **prep time** 5 minutes
cooking time 30 minutes

1 **package (7¼-ounce) macaroni and cheese mix, Kraft®**
1 **tablespoon Mexican seasoning, McCormick®**
¾ **cup shredded Mexican cheese blend, Kraft®**

1. Preheat oven to 350 degrees F.

2. Make macaroni and cheese according to package directions. Transfer to a medium-size baking dish or casserole dish.

3. Sprinkle Mexican seasoning over top of macaroni and cheese. Sprinkle cheese blend over top to cover. Bake for 5 minutes or until cheese is melted.

Italian-Style Macaroni and Cheese

servings 4 **prep time** 5 minutes
cooking time 30 minutes

1 **package (7¼-ounce) macaroni and cheese mix, Kraft®**
2 **tablespoons butter**
1 **cup Italian-style bread crumbs, Progresso®**

1. Preheat oven to 350 degrees F.

2. Make macaroni and cheese according to package directions. Transfer to a medium-size baking dish or casserole dish.

3. Melt butter in a medium bowl on low (25% power) in the microwave. Add bread crumbs and toss to coat with butter. Sprinkle bread crumb mixture over top of macaroni and cheese. Bake for 10 to 15 minutes or until browned on top.

Macaroni and Cheese with Broccoli

servings 4 **prep time** 5 minutes
cooking time 30 minutes

1 **package (7¼-ounce) macaroni and cheese mix, Kraft®**
1 **to 1½ cups leftover broccoli florets**

1. Preheat oven to 350 degrees F.

2. Make macaroni and cheese according to package directions. Add broccoli and stir to combine. Transfer to a medium-size casserole dish. Bake about 10 minutes or until heated through.

Chunky Chili

2   tablespoons butter
1   medium sweet onion, very finely chopped
1½ pounds ground beef
2   cans (15 ounces each) red kidney beans, drained, **S&W**®
1   jar (26-ounce) marinara sauce, **Newman's Own**®
1   package (1.25-ounce) chili seasoning, **Schilling**®, minus 1 tablespoon
    reserved for Chili Rolls (see recipe below)
   Shredded cheese, for garnish
   Sour cream, for garnish
   Minced chives, for garnish

1. In a large skillet over medium heat, melt butter. Add onion and saute until softened. Crumble in the beef and cook until browned. Stir in beans and marinara sauce. Stir in chili seasoning. Reduce heat and simmer for 15 minutes. Ladle into soup bowls and garnish with cheese, sour cream, and chives.

Serving Idea: Serve with Chili Rolls (below).

Chili Rolls

1   stick butter
1   tablespoon chili seasoning, **Schilling**® (see recipe, above)
1   package (12-count) brown-and-serve rolls, **Van de Kamp's**®

1. In a medium saucepan over medium heat, melt butter. Stir in chili seasoning. Brush tops of rolls with chili butter, then place rolls on a baking sheet covered with foil. Bake according to package directions, until golden brown, about 15 minutes.

Cherry Almond Crumble

servings 4 prep time 15 minutes
baking time 20 minutes

Nonstick cooking spray, PAM®
1 **cup cherry pie filling or topping, Comstock More Fruit®**
1 **cup cherry preserves, Smucker's®**
¼ **cup dried cherries**
1½ **teaspoons pure almond extract, McCormick®**
1 **cup quick-cooking oats, Quaker®**
½ **cup dark brown sugar, C&H®**
½ **cup sliced almonds**
1 **teaspoon ground cinnamon, McCormick®**
5 **tablespoons butter, melted**
Whipped topping or sour cream

1. Preheat oven to 400 degrees F. Spray four 8-ounce ramekins or custard cups with cooking spray. In a large bowl, combine pie filling, preserves, dried cherries, and almond extract. Spoon cherry filling into prepared ramekins. Place ramekins on a baking sheet.

2. In a medium bowl, toss together oats, brown sugar, almonds, and cinnamon. Drizzle melted butter over mixture and stir to moisten. Sprinkle topping over cherry filling. Bake about 20 minutes or until topping is golden and filling is bubbling. Serve warm with whipped topping.

Apple Pie Napoleon

servings 8 prep time 20 minutes
baking time 50 minutes + 15 minutes

1 **Dutch apple crumb pie, Mrs. Smith's®**
1 **sheet frozen puff pastry, Pepperidge Farms®**
All-purpose flour, for dusting
2 **cups frozen whipped topping, thawed, Cool Whip®**
2 **teaspoons cinnamon sugar**
1 **package (3 ounces) cream cheese, softened, Philadelphia®**
¾ **cup powdered sugar, sifted, C&H®**
2 **tablespoons caramel cream liqueur, Paul Masson®**

1. Bake apple pie according to package directions, about 50 minutes. Let cool. Once cooled, break up pie with a fork.

2. Thaw pastry sheet at room temperature for 30 minutes. Preheat oven to 400 degrees F. On a flour-dusted surface, unfold sheet. Cut pastry into 3 strips along fold marks. Place strips 2 inches apart on baking sheet. Bake for 15 minutes or until golden. Remove from baking sheet; cool on wire rack.

3. In a small bowl, combine whipped topping and cinnamon sugar; set aside. In a small mixing bowl, beat cream cheese and powdered sugar with an electric mixer on low speed until light and fluffy. Add liqueur; beat until smooth.

4. Place 1 baked pastry sheet on a platter. With the back of a fork, gently push down center of pastry creating a trough for filling. Spoon in apple pie pieces; spread 1 cup whipped topping mixture over top. Repeat layers. Top with third pastry sheet. Drizzle with cream cheese glaze and serve.

Coffee Chocolate Brownies with Mocha Icing

servings 12 **prep time** 10 minutes
baking time 30 minutes

Brownies
- ½ **cup butter, softened**
- ⅓ **cup packed light brown sugar, C&H®**
- 1 **tablespoon instant coffee crystals, Maxwell House®**
- 1 **box (18.25-ounce) devil's food cake mix, Betty Crocker® SuperMoist®**
- 1 **large egg**
- ¼ **cup water**
- 1 **teaspoon pure almond extract, McCormick®**
- 1 **cup slivered almonds, toasted**

Icing
- 1 **stick butter, softened**
- 4 **cups powdered sugar, C&H®**
- ½ **cup chocolate syrup, Hershey's®**
- 1½ **teaspoons instant espresso powder**

1. Preheat oven to 350 degrees F. Grease a 9×13-inch baking pan.

2. For brownies, in a large mixing bowl, combine butter, brown sugar, and coffee. Beat with an electric mixer on medium speed until light and fluffy. Add cake mix, egg, water, and almond extract and beat until smooth. Stir in almonds.

3. Spoon batter into prepared pan and spread to edges. Bake for 30 to 35 minutes until toothpick inserted in center comes out clean. Cool completely in pan on cooling rack.

4. For icing, in a small mixing bowl, beat butter with an electric mixer on low speed until smooth. While beating, add powdered sugar 1 cup at a time. When sugar is incorporated, beat on medium speed until light and fluffy. Beat in chocolate syrup and espresso powder until smooth.

5. Let brownies cool. Once cooled, spread brownies with icing and cut into squares.

Apple Pie Punch

2 cups apple juice or cider
4 ounces spiced rum, *Myers's®*
2 ounces cinnamon schnapps, *Goldschlager®*
  Ice cubes
1 red apple, sliced, for garnish
  Cinnamon sticks, for garnish

1. In a pitcher, combine apple juice, rum, and schnapps. Serve punch over ice cubes and garnish with red apple slices and cinnamon sticks.

Brick House Mary

6 ounces tomato juice, *Campbell's®*
2 ounces vodka, *Absolut® Peppar*
6 dashes Worcestershire sauce, or to taste, *Lea & Perrins®*
½ teaspoon prepared horseradish, or to taste, *Morehouse®*
  Celery salt to taste
  Freshly ground pepper to taste
  Jalapeño juice (from jarred jalapeños)
  Whole jalapeño, for garnish
  Lemon slice, for garnish

1. Fill a 12-ounce highball glass with ice. Add all ingredients, except whole jalapeño and lemon slice. Mix by pouring back and forth between two glasses.

2. Pour into a glass rimmed with celery salt. Garnish with jalapeño and lemon slice.

Light & Healthful

The older I get, the more health conscious I become and the more I find myself having to constantly balance my love for good food with my desire to be fit. When it comes to eating, many people are of the "no fat, no point" persuasion. That's what I thought, until I came up with these light, luscious recipes that say good riddance to bad habits—and look great doing it!

From full-flavored entrées to rich desserts and refreshing cocktails, this chapter introduces food with a new attitude. A fit and trim version of more sinful concoctions, every recipe uses a creative mix of ingredients, seasonings, and savvy substitutions to maximize flavor and taste and minimize fat and calories. Whether you're watching cholesterol, salt, sugar, or simply your waistline, they're a hassle-free way to achieve a healthy new you.

The Recipes

Sandra in her garden.

Crab Louie Salad

servings 4
prep time 15 minutes

calories 332 **fat** 19 grams **saturated fat** 3 grams **cholesterol** 189 milligrams

2   **cans (6 ounces each) lump crabmeat, drained,** *Geisha*®, **or 12 ounces fresh crabmeat**
1/3 cup bacon and tomato twist mayonnaise, *Best Foods*®
1/4 cup sweet pickle relish, *Del Monte*®
1   medium head green leaf lettuce, chopped
1   medium head iceberg lettuce, chopped
1   small green bell pepper, sliced into 1/4-inch rings
1   medium cucumber, sliced 1/4 inch thick
1   tomato, sliced into 8 wedges
1/2 can (1/2 of a 6-ounce can) ripe olives (whole and pitted), drained, *Lindsay*®
2   hard-boiled eggs, quartered lengthwise

1. In a medium bowl, combine crabmeat, mayonnaise, and relish. Set aside.

2. On a large chilled platter or in a chilled bowl, combine the two types of lettuce. Spoon the crabmeat mixture into the center. Arrange the remaining ingredients around the crabmeat mixture.

Lobster Wraps

servings 4 to 6 **prep time** 15 minutes
chilling time 1 hour

calories 307 **fat** 17 grams **saturated fat** 2 grams **cholesterol** 17 milligrams

1   package (8-ounce) imitation lobster nuggets, *Louis Kemp*®
1   avocado, peeled, pitted, and diced
1   cup diced, seeded tomato
1/4 cup pepita-cilantro Caesar dressing, *El Torito*®
4   cups salad mix, *Ready Pac*®
2   jalapeño-cilantro tortillas (12-inch), *Mission*®

1. In a medium bowl, combine lobster, avocado, tomato, and dressing. Pile equal amounts of salad mix on tortillas, spreading to within 1 inch of edges. Top with lobster mixture. Roll tortillas up tightly and wrap in plastic wrap. Chill at least 1 hour. Remove plastic wrap and slice into 1-inch rounds.

Smoked Salmon and Avocado Stacks

servings 4
prep time 20 minutes

calories 316 **fat** 16 grams **saturated fat** 3 grams **cholesterol** 13 milligrams

1 **package (8-ounce) lox smoked salmon**
  Kosher salt and freshly ground pepper
  Champagne vinaigrette, *Girards®*
  Croutons
3 **ripe avocados**
½ **lemon, juiced**
  Pinch prepared wasabi
  Fresh chives, cut into small pieces, for garnish

1. Place a 3-inch ring mold on a plate. Layer 2 to 3 pieces of salmon in the mold. Season salmon to taste with salt and pepper. Sprinkle a few dashes of vinaigrette over the salmon and top with croutons.

2. Peel, pit, and thinly slice the avocados. Squeeze lemon juice over avocado slices to prevent discoloration. In a small bowl, gently toss avocados with wasabi. Place 3 to 4 slices of the avocado on top of the croutons.

3. Repeat each layer. Remove the ring mold and garnish with chives. Repeat to make a total of 4 stacks.

Herb and Rib-Eye Salad

servings 2 **prep time** 15 minutes
cooking time 7 minutes

Not everyone wants more in life; some of us want less, especially when it comes to fat and calories. This salad-as-a-meal entrée is the poster dish for a new way of eating, that is, beefing up taste while cutting fat. If you're trying to eat less red meat or want to experiment with variations, use sliced pork roast, chicken, or seafood. All are amazing alternatives.

calories 314 **fat** 19 grams **saturated fat** 4 grams **cholesterol** 55 milligrams

1 **rib-eye steak, 1 inch thick**
 Salt and pepper
1 **tablespoon canola oil,** *Wesson*®
1 **head butter lettuce, leaves removed and torn**
¼ **cup fresh thyme leaves**
¼ **cup snipped fresh chives**
¼ **cup fresh tarragon leaves**
¼ **cup torn fresh basil leaves**
2 **roma tomatoes, seeded and diced**
 Balsamic vinaigrette, *Newman's Own*®

1. Season the steak generously on both sides with salt and pepper, patting the seasoning into the meat.

2. Heat a large heavy skillet, preferably cast iron, over medium heat. Add oil to hot skillet. When oil is hot, add the steak and cook until seared and well-crusted on 1 side, about 4 minutes. Turn and cook 3 minutes more for medium-rare or 4 minutes more for medium.

3. Transfer steak to cutting board and let rest, covered loosely with foil.

4. Meanwhile, combine lettuce and herbs and divide between 2 plates.

5. Thinly slice steak across the grain, trimming away fat. Arrange steak slices on top of greens. Sprinkle with chopped tomatoes and drizzle with vinaigrette.

Variation: Substitute red grapes and sunflower seeds for tomatoes.

Flounder with Red Pepper Cream Sauce and Asparagus Risotto

servings 4 **prep time** 15 minutes
cooking time 20 minutes

These flounder fillets star as catch of the day any day, but they're also impressive enough for company. Topped with a roasted red pepper Alfredo sauce, they're a dieter's delight—rich, creamy, and completely satisfying. Pair with a side of fresh asparagus risotto for a quick-to-the-table meal.

calories 474 **fat** 13 grams **saturated fat** 4 grams **cholesterol** 113 milligrams

- 2 **tablespoons extra virgin olive oil, _Bertolli®_**
- 4 **flounder fillets (8 ounces each)**
  Salt and pepper
- 1 **pound asparagus, trimmed and cut into 1-inch lengths**
- 1 **box (5.5-ounce) garden vegetable risotto mix, _Buitoni®_**
- ½ **cup jarred roasted red peppers, _Mancini®_**
- ½ **cup light Alfredo pasta sauce**
  Fresh basil sprigs, for garnish

1. Preheat oven to 450 degrees F.

2. Pour oil into a 13×9-inch baking dish. Arrange fish in dish, folding the ends under the middle to create little pockets. Sprinkle fish with salt and pepper to taste. Roast for 5 minutes. Add asparagus to dish; roast for 5 to 7 minutes longer or until fish flakes easily when tested with a fork. Remove from oven and keep fish warm. Remove asparagus from dish and set aside.

3. Prepare risotto according to package directions; stir in the roasted asparagus.

4. Meanwhile, in a blender, puree roasted peppers and alfredo sauce. Transfer mixture to a small saucepan and warm over medium heat.

5. Serve fish topped with sauce and accompanied by risotto. Garnish with fresh basil sprigs.

Mango-Marinated Swordfish and Fruit Salsa

servings 4 **prep time** 15 minutes
marinate time 1 hour **cooking time** 10 minutes

calories 329 **fat** 14 grams **saturated fat** 2 grams **cholesterol** 66 milligrams

Marinade
- ¼ **cup mango nectar**
- 1 **tablespoon canola oil,** *Wesson*®
- 2 **tablespoons balsamic vinegar**
- 1 **teaspoon ground ginger,** *McCormick*®
- 1 **teaspoon pepper**
- 1 **teaspoon red pepper flakes,** *McCormick*®
- ¼ **teaspoon ground nutmeg,** *McCormick*®

- 4 **swordfish steaks (6 to 8 ounce each)**

Salsa
- 1 **can (15.25-ounce) tropical fruit salad, drained,** *Dole*®
- 1 **green onion, finely chopped**
- ½ **lime, juiced**
- 1 **small jalapeño, membrane removed, seeded, and minced**
- 1 **tablespoon finely chopped fresh cilantro**
   Salt to taste

- 1 **tablespoon canola oil,** *Wesson*®

1. In small bowl, whisk together marinade ingredients. Pour into a resealable plastic bag. Add swordfish; seal bag. Refrigerate 1 hour, turning bag occasionally.

2. For salsa, chop up drained fruit. In a medium bowl, combine fruit and remaining salsa ingredients. Cover and refrigerate while fish marinates.

3. In a large skillet over medium-high heat, heat 2 tablespoons oil. Cook fish about 5 minutes per side or until fish flakes. Serve topped with salsa.

Vegetables with Broccoli Lemon Sauce

servings 8 **prep time** 10 minutes
cooking time 15 minutes

calories 126 **fat** 6 grams **saturated fat** 1 grams **cholesterol** 7 milligrams

- 12 **small red potatoes, cut into quarters**
- 1 **large green or red bell pepper, cut into** ¼-inch rings
- 2 **cups broccoli florets**
- 1 **can (10¾-ounce) cream of broccoli soup (98% fat-free),** *Campbell's*®
- ½ **cup low-fat mayonnaise,** *Best Foods*®
- 4 **green onions, finely chopped**
- 1 **tablespoon fresh lemon juice, or** *ReaLemon*®
- ¼ **teaspoon dried thyme leaves, crushed,** *McCormick*®

1. In a saucepan, combine potatoes with water to cover. Bring to boil. Cover, reduce heat, and simmer 10 minutes. Add pepper and broccoli. Cook 5 minutes more or until vegetables are tender.

2. In second saucepan, combine soup, mayonnaise, onions, lemon juice, and thyme. Heat through and serve over vegetables.

Ale-Poached Halibut

servings 2 **prep time** 10 minutes
cooking time 8+ minutes

calories 275 **fat** 5 grams **saturated fat** 1 gram **cholesterol** 54 milligrams

- **2** **halibut fillets (6 to 8 ounces each)**
- **Water**
- **1** **bottle (12-ounce) ale-style beer**
- **2** **teaspoons seafood seasoning,** *Old Bay*®
- **½** **lemon, juiced**
- **1** **teaspoon salt**
- **10** **whole peppercorns,** *McCormick*®

Serving Idea: Serve over Apple Rice Pilaf with Toasted Almonds (below).

1. Place the fish in poacher or a skillet with 4-inch sides. Add enough water to cover fish. Remove fish from water and set aside.

2. Add remaining ingredients to pan. Bring to boil.

3. Reduce heat to simmer. Return fish to pan and poach about 8 minutes per 1-inch thickness of fish or until fish flakes easily when tested with a fork.

Apple Rice Pilaf with Toasted Almonds

servings 6 **prep time** 5 minutes
cooking time 10 minutes

calories 222 **fat** 5 grams **saturated fat** 1 gram **cholesterol** 5 milligrams

- **1** **tablespoon butter**
- **¼** **onion, finely chopped**
- **¼** **Golden Delicious apple, finely chopped**
- **2** **cups apple juice**
- **2** **cups long grain instant rice,** *Uncle Ben's*®
- **¼** **cup slivered almonds, toasted**

1. In a medium saucepan over medium heat, melt butter. Add onion and apple, and saute until soft. Add apple juice and bring to boil.

2. Stir in rice. Cover and remove from heat. Let sit for 5 minutes. Stir in almonds.

Blackened Cajun Catfish

servings 4 **prep time** 10 minutes
cooking time 15 minutes

calories 245 **fat** 15 grams **saturated fat** 4 grams **cholesterol** 56 milligrams

- 1½ **tablespoons extra virgin olive oil,** *Bertolli*®
- 2 **cloves garlic, smashed**
- 2 **tablespoons Cajun seasoning,** *McCormick*®
- 1 **teaspoon poultry seasoning,** *McCormick*®
- 1 **pound catfish fillets**
- ½ **cup white wine**
- 2 **tablespoons fresh lemon juice, or** *ReaLemon*®
- 1 **teaspoon butter**

1. In a large skillet over medium-low heat, heat oil. Add garlic cloves and cook until golden brown. Remove and discard garlic cloves. Remove skillet from heat.

2. In a small bowl, combine Cajun and poultry seasonings; set aside.

3. Rinse fish and pat dry with paper towels. Sprinkle both sides of fish with seasoning mix.

4. Return skillet to medium-high heat. When oil is hot, add fish, presentation side (the side against the bone) down. Cook fish for 5 minutes per side or until fish flakes easily when tested with a fork. Transfer fish to a plate.

5. Deglaze pan with white wine and lemon juice. Bring to boil. Reduce heat and simmer for 2 minutes. Swirl butter into sauce. Pour over fish.

Dirty Rice

servings 4 **prep time** 10 minutes
cooking time 30 minutes

calories 198 **fat** 4 grams **saturated fat** 1 gram **cholesterol** 0 milligrams

- 1 **tablespoon extra virgin olive oil,** *Bertolli*®
- ¼ **cup finely diced onion**
- ¼ **cup finely diced celery**
- ½ **green bell pepper, finely diced**
- 2⅓ **cups reduced-sodium chicken broth,** *Swanson*®
- ¾ **teaspoon poultry seasoning,** *McCormick*®
- 1 **box (6-ounce) long grain and wild rice mix,** *Uncle Ben's*®

1. In a medium skillet, heat oil over medium heat. Add onion, celery, and pepper to hot oil. Saute until vegetables are soft but not brown.

2. Add broth and poultry seasoning; bring to boil. Add rice and seasoning packet. Cover, reduce heat to low, and simmer for 25 minutes. Fluff with fork and serve.

Citrus Balsamic Glazed Salmon

servings 4 **prep time** 10 minutes
baking time 15 minutes

Salmon, an excellent source of protein and omega-3 fatty acids, provides disease-countering benefits that protect your heart. The richness of the fish is balanced by a refreshing vinaigrette made with orange juice, brown sugar, and balsamic vinegar. It tastes as good as it is nutritious, and it goes from fridge to table in less than 30 minutes.

calories 406 **fat** 24 grams **saturated fat** 4 grams **cholesterol** 102 milligrams

8   salmon fillets, $^3/_4$ inch thick (about $1^1/_2$ pounds total)
     Salt and pepper
$1^1/_2$ tablespoons olive oil, *Bertolli*®
3   tablespoons balsamic vinegar
$1^1/_2$ tablespoons cornstarch
1   tablespoon brown sugar, *C&H*®
1   tablespoon orange juice
1   can (14-ounce) seasoned chicken broth, *Swanson*®

1. Preheat oven to 350 degrees F.

2. Rub salmon with salt and pepper to taste. Place salmon in a shallow 2-quart baking dish. Drizzle with oil. Bake for 15 minutes or until fish flakes easily when tested with a fork.

3. Meanwhile, in a medium saucepan, whisk together vinegar, cornstarch, brown sugar, and orange juice. Whisk in broth and bring to boil. Reduce heat to simmer, stirring until the mixture thickens.

4. Arrange salmon on serving platter and spoon sauce over top.

Serving Idea: Serve salmon on bed of white rice.

Strawberry Meringue Cake

servings 12 **prep time** 20 minutes
baking time 50 minutes
assembling time 15 minutes

calories 179 **fat** 2 grams **saturated fat** 2 grams **cholesterol** 1 milligram

6	egg whites
¼	teaspoon cream of tartar, *McCormick®*
⅛	teaspoon salt
1¼	cups sugar, *C&H®*
1½	teaspoons strawberry extract, *McCormick®*
1¾	cups nonfat milk
1	box (3.4-ounce) lemon instant pudding and pie filling mix, *Jell-O®*
2	teaspoon finely minced lemon zest
1	cup sliced fresh strawberries
1	container (8-ounce) low-fat frozen whipped topping, thawed, *Cool Whip®*
	Fresh mint sprigs and raspberries (see photo, left), for garnish

1. Preheat oven to 275 degrees F. Line 2 baking sheets with parchment paper. Draw two 8-inch circles on each sheet of parchment. Turn parchment over, marked side down, on pan. Set aside.

2. For meringues, in a large bowl, beat egg whites, cream of tartar, and salt with an electric mixer on high speed until soft peaks form. Gradually add sugar and strawberry extract until whites form stiff, but not dry, peaks. Divide egg mixture among 4 circles on parchment. Spread to edges of circles. Bake for 50 minutes. Turn oven off, leaving meringues in oven to dry.

3. For lemon filling, whisk together milk, lemon pudding mix, and lemon zest for 2 minutes until filling starts to thicken. Cover with plastic wrap and chill at least 1 hour. For strawberry filling, gently fold strawberries into half container of whipped topping. Cover with plastic wrap and refrigerate.

4. Assemble dessert just before serving. Place 1 meringue on cake plate. Spread half the lemon filling over meringue. Top with another meringue and spread with strawberry filling. Top with third meringue and remaining lemon filling. Place last meringue on top; spread with remaining whipped topping. Garnish with mint sprigs and raspberries.

Whipped cream-filled raspberries add a playful finish. Spoon whipped topping into a plastic bag, make a small snip at one of the tips of the bag. Pipe topping into the centers of fresh berries and sprinkle them over top of the cake.

Sorbet Shooters

servings 10
prep time 15 minutes

calories 96 **fat** 0 grams **saturated fat** 0 grams **cholesterol** 0 milligrams

1	pint sorbet
¾	cup flavored liqueur

1. Using a melon baller, place small scoops of sorbet into each shot glass (only 1 flavor per glass). Top sorbet with about 1 tablespoon of matching flavored liqueur.

Angel Food Cake
with Mixed Berries

servings 8
prep time 5 minutes

calories 229 **fat** 1 grams **saturated fat** 0 grams **cholesterol** 0 milligrams

- 1 **package (1 pint) fresh strawberries**
- 1 **package (½ pint) raspberries**
- 1 **package (½ pint) blackberries**
- 1 **package (½ pint) blueberries**
- 2 **tablespoons sugar, C&H®**
- 1 **purchased (10- to 12-ounce) angel food cake**

1. In a large bowl, combine berries and sugar, mashing slightly to make juice. Spoon berry mixture over top of angel food cake or over slices. Garnish with additional fresh berries, if desired.

Berry Frothy Burst

servings 2
prep time 5 minutes

calories 142 **fat** 2 grams **saturated fat** 0 grams **cholesterol** 0 milligrams

- 1 **cup frozen mixed berries**
- 1 **cup orange juice**
- 3½ **ounces silken (soft) tofu (¼ of 14-ounce package)**
- ½ **banana**

1. Place all ingredients in a blender. Blend until smooth.

Slow Cooking

The low-tech slow cooker is one of the hottest new (and at the same time old) appliances in happening homes. It cooks all day so you don't have to. With two young daughters and a business to run, my friend Hilary is always looking for ways to stretch her time ... and budget. She gets up in the morning, throws an inexpensive roast in the slow cooker, adds vegetables, broth, and seasoning, replaces the lid, and forgets about it. By five o'clock, the smell of dinner is wafting through the house. It tastes like it took her all day, but the meal actually came together in seven minutes.

Inspired, I set about creating slow cooker recipes for every taste and every occasion, from every-night dinners to potluck parties. You'll find classic family favorites such as chicken and pasta, and savory soups and chili to warm a crowd on a cold day. The slow cooker puts fast food at your fingertips, serving up wholesome, homey meals at the touch of a button.

The Recipes

Safe Slow Cooking

Follow these basic guidelines for no-fail slow cooking:

- Cooking time depends on the setting you choose. The recipes that cook for 4 hours on high will take 7 to 8 hours on low. If you want food to cook all day, select the low setting.
- A slow cooker needs liquid to cook. Add juice, broth, wine or spirits instead of water to enhance flavor. Because wine and liquors evaporate during cooking leaving only flavor, these dishes are family-friendly.
- To avoid cracking the pot, put cold ingredients into a cold slow cooker and warm ingredients into a preheated slow cooker. Always follow the manufacturer's instructions for best results.

167

French
Onion Soup

servings 8 **prep time** 5 minutes
cooking time 4 hours (High) or 8 hours (Low)

5 cups sliced onions
2 cans (14 ounces each) low-sodium beef broth, *Swanson*®
2 cans (10 ounces each) beef consommé, *Campbell's*®
1 packet (0.9-ounce) onion soup mix, *Lipton*®
8 slices French bread
1 cup shredded Gruyère cheese

1. Combine onions, broth, consommé, and soup mix in a 3½- or 4-quart slow cooker. Cover and cook on high-heat setting for 4 hours or low-heat setting for 8 hours.

2. Ladle soup into 8 soup bowls arranged on a baking sheet. Top each with a slice of French bread. Sprinkle 2 tablespoons of cheese over each bread slice. Put soup bowls under a broiler until cheese is melted.

Herb
Tortellini Soup

servings 8 **prep time** 10 minutes
cooking time 3 hours (High) or 7 hours (Low)

3 cans (14.5-ounce) low-sodium chicken broth, *Swanson*®
1 can (28-ounce) crushed tomatoes, *Hunt's*®
1 can (11-ounce) sweet corn (no added salt), *Green Giant*®
1 package (10-ounce) frozen cut-leaf spinach
1 small red onion, diced
1 zucchini, diced
½ cup chopped fresh herbs (parsley, thyme, oregano, basil)
1 tablespoon bottled minced garlic, *McCormick*®
1 tablespoon Italian salad dressing mix, *Good Season's*®
½ teaspoon red pepper flakes, *McCormick*®
   Salt and pepper to taste
1 package (8-ounce) cheese tortellini, *Barilla*®

1. Combine all ingredients, except tortellini, in a 3½- to 4-quart slow cooker. Cover and cook on high-heat setting for 3 hours or low-heat setting for 7 hours.

2. Add tortellini and continue cooking for 1 hour. (If cooking on low-heat setting, turn to high-heat setting to cook tortellini.)

Creamy Chicken Noodle Soup

servings 8 prep time 10 minutes
cooking time 3 hours (High) or 8 hours (Low)

1 store-bought roasted chicken
1 cup diced onion
1 cup diced celery
1 cup diced carrots
4 cans (14 ounces each) low-sodium chicken broth, *Swanson*®
2 cans (10¾ ounces each) condensed cream of mushroom soup with roasted garlic, *Campbell's*®
2 teaspoons fines herbes*
Salt and pepper
2 cups egg noodles, cooked, *American Beauty*®

1. Remove skin from roasted chicken and shred meat from bone. Place chicken, onion, celery, and carrots in a 3½- to 4-quart slow cooker. Stir in broth, soup, and fines herbes. Season to taste with salt and pepper. Cover and cook on high-heat setting for 3 to 4 hours or low-heat setting for 8 to 9 hours.

2. When soup is done, stir in cooked egg noodles and heat through. Adjust seasonings and serve.

***Note:** Fines herbes are a classic blend of herbs that usually consists of chervil, chives, parsley, and tarragon. You'll find it preblended in the spice section of the grocery store.

Mexican Meatball Rice Soup

servings 8 prep time 5 minutes
cooking time 3 hours (High) or 8 hours (Low)

1 can (7-ounce) diced green chiles, *Ortega*®
2 cans (14.5 ounces each) diced tomatoes, *Hunt's*®
2 cans (14 ounces each) low-sodium beef broth, *Swanson*®
2 cans (14 ounces each) low-sodium chicken broth, *Swanson*®
16 ounces frozen meatballs
1 medium white onion, chopped
½ cup chopped fresh cilantro
½ cup converted rice, *Uncle Ben's*®
2 teaspoons dried oregano, *McCormick*®
Salt and pepper to taste

1. Combine all ingredients in a 4- to 5-quart slow cooker. Cover and cook on high-heat setting for 3 to 4 hours or low-heat setting for 8 to 9 hours.

Serving Idea: Serve piping hot with extra chopped cilantro, lime wedges, and chopped onions.

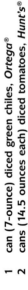

Beefy Stuffed Peppers

servings 6 **prep time** 10 minutes
cooking time 3 hours (High) or 6 hours (Low)

The only way this recipe could get any simpler is if it were to cook itself—which it practically does! It's a busy parent's best friend, a nutritious family favorite that kids love. The meatloaf-and-rice-style stuffing is cooked and served in hollowed-out peppers that serve as edible individual casseroles. You can use peppers of any color, but I prefer red and yellow. They're sweeter than others and make a more colorful presentation.

6   **red or yellow bell peppers**
1½ **pounds lean ground beef**
1   **can (11-ounce) Mexican-style corn, *Green Giant*®**
1   **can (7-ounce) sliced ripe olives, *Early California*®**
1   **cup shredded Mexican cheese blend, *Sargento*®**
½ **cup converted rice, *Uncle Ben's*®**
1   **packet (1.0-ounce) taco seasoning, *Lawry's*®**
1   **can (10¾-ounce) condensed tomato soup, *Campbell's*®**
1   **can (10-ounce) diced tomatoes, *Rotel*®**
¼ **cup shredded Mexican cheese blend, *Sargento*®**

1. Cut tops off peppers. Remove stems, seeds, and cores from peppers. Dice pepper tops.

2. In a large bowl, combine beef, corn, olives, 1 cup cheese, the rice, taco seasoning, and diced pepper tops. Stuff peppers with equal portions of meat mixture. Place stuffed bell peppers in a 4- to 5-quart slow cooker.

3. In another bowl, combine soup and tomatoes. Pour over stuffed peppers in slow cooker. Top peppers with ¼ cup shredded cheese. Cover and cook on high-heat setting for 3 to 4 hours or low-heat setting for 6 to 7 hours.

Tip: A Bundt pan is a creative—and practical—way to serve stuffed peppers or to conveniently transport them to a potluck dinner.

Dr. Pepper® Pork Roast

servings 8 **prep time** 10 minutes
cooking time 3 hours (High) or 8 hours (Low)
stand 10 minutes

My aunt Peggy loves Dr. Pepper®, it's the only thing she drinks! So this pork roast is a recipe I created for her, and it's absolutely delicious, by the way, it tastes just as good made with Diet Dr. Pepper.®

- 2 medium onions, sliced
- 2 tablespoons canola oil, *Wesson*®
- 1 4-pound pork loin roast
-   Salt and pepper
- 5 whole cloves, *McCormick*®
- 2 sticks cinnamon, *McCormick*®
- 1 whole bay leaf, *McCormick*®
- 1 can (12-ounce) *Dr. Pepper*®
- 1½ cups dried apricot halves, *Sunsweet*®
- 1½ cups dried plums (pitted prunes), *Sunsweet*®

1. Place sliced onions in a 3½- to 4-quart slow cooker. In a large skillet, heat oil over medium-high heat. Season pork roast with salt and pepper. Brown roast on all sides in skillet. Place browned roast in cooker on top of onions.

2. Add cloves, cinnamon sticks, and bay leaf to cooker. Pour Dr. Pepper® over roast and top roast with dried fruit. Cover and cook on high-heat setting for 3 to 4 hours or low-heat setting for 8 to 9 hours or until internal temperature of roast is 160 degrees F.

3. Remove roast from cooker and let rest for 10 minutes. Use a slotted spoon to remove onion, fruit, and spices from cooker; discard spices. Skim fat from sauce in cooker. Slice roast and serve topped with onions, fruit, and sauce.

Chicken with Mushrooms and Artichokes

servings 6 **prep time** 10 minutes
cooking time 3 hours (High) or 7 hours (Low)

Eating (and enjoying) your vegetables has never been easier. Simply toss them in the slow cooker with chicken before you leave for work and come home to a delectable dinner. It's a sophisticated way to present a wholesome "Mommy Meal" or a cook-and-carry treat for grownup gatherings. Make a potful for nearly effortless entertaining. It'll spread a welcoming aroma throughout the house.

2   tablespoons extra-virgin olive oil, *Bertolli®*
4   pounds chicken breasts and thighs, rinsed and patted dry
    Salt and pepper
2   cans (10³/₄ ounces each) condensed golden mushroom soup,
    Campbell's®
2   teaspoons Italian seasoning, *McCormick®*
1   packet (1.5-ounce) four-cheese sauce mix, *Knorr®*
10 ounces mushrooms, sliced
8   ounces frozen artichoke hearts
1   cup frozen chopped onions
1   medium red bell pepper, finely chopped

1. Heat oil in large skillet over medium-high heat. Season chicken with salt and pepper to taste. Working in batches, brown chicken on both sides in skillet. Transfer to plate and set aside.

2. In a medium bowl, combine soup, Italian seasoning, and cheese sauce mix. Set aside.

3. Combine mushrooms, artichoke hearts, onions, and bell pepper in a 4- or 5-quart slow cooker. Add browned chicken and any accumulated juices. Pour soup mixture over chicken.

4. Cover and cook on high-heat setting for 3 to 4 hours or low-heat setting for 7 to 8 hours.

Beef Roast with Tomato Madeira Sauce

servings 6 **prep time** 10 minutes
cooking time 8 hours (Low)

2   tablespoons extra-virgin olive oil, *Bertolli*®
1   3-pound beef rump roast
    Salt and pepper
1½ cups roasted garlic and herb tomato sauce, *Prego*®
¾   cup Madeira wine
1   teaspoon bottled minced garlic, *McCormick*®
1½ cups frozen pearl onions
1   cup frozen sliced carrots

1. In a large skillet, heat oil over medium-high heat. Season roast with salt and pepper. Brown roast on all sides in skillet. Transfer to plate and set aside.

2. In a medium bowl, combine tomato sauce, Madeira, and garlic. Set aside.

3. Place onions and carrots in a 3½- to 4-quart slow cooker. Add roast and any accumulated juices. Pour sauce mixture over roast.

4. Cover and cook on low-heat setting for 8 hours.

Pork Roast with Sherry Cream Sauce

servings 8 **prep time** 10 minutes
cooking time 3 hours (High) or 8 hours (Low)
stand time 5 to 10 minutes

Pork roast is classic family food, an old favorite that stirs good memories with every bite. This version has a French twist: a simmered-in sauce of creamy sherry seasoned with fragrant herbes de Provence. Give it continental flair with a très chic garnish of peppers and squash and a delicate white wine to counterbalance the herbs.

- 1 large onion, sliced
- 8 ounces mushrooms, sliced
- 2 tablespoons extra-virgin olive oil, *Bertolli®*
- 1 3½-pound pork shoulder roast, rinsed and patted dry
  Salt and pepper
- 2 cans (10¾ ounces each) condensed cream of mushroom soup, *Campbell's®*
- 1 cup sherry wine
- 2 teaspoons herbes de Provence*, *McCormick® Gourmet Collection®*
- 1 teaspoon bottled minced garlic, *McCormick®*

1. Place onion and mushrooms in a 3½- to 4-quart slow cooker.

2. In a large skillet, heat oil over medium-high heat. Season roast with salt and pepper to taste. Brown roast on all sides in skillet. Transfer to slow cooker.

3. In a medium bowl, combine soup, sherry, herbes de Provence, and garlic. Pour soup mixture over roast.

4. Cover and cook on high-heat setting for 3 to 4 hours or low-heat setting for 8 to 9 hours or until internal temperature of roast is 160 degrees F. Remove roast from slow cooker and let rest for 5 to 10 minutes.

*Note: Herbes de Provence is a blend of dry herbs most commonly used in Southern France. It usually contains basil, fennel seeds, lavender, marjoram, rosemary, sage, summer savory, and thyme.

Beer BBQ Chicken

servings 8 **prep time** 10 minutes
cooking time 3 hours (High) or 7 hours (Low)

Every meal is a happy hour with this hit-the-spot dish that goes down as easy as a bottle of your favorite brew. A tantalizing blend of cool, refreshing beer and hot, smoky barbeque sauce, it is the meal to make when you want something simple yet sensational. Spoon extra sauce over each serving to intensify the flavor.

1 teaspoon canola oil, *Wesson*®
4 pounds chicken breasts and thighs, rinsed and patted dry
   Salt and pepper
2 medium onions, cut into wedges
1 cup dark beer or ale
1½ cups barbecue sauce

1. In a large skillet, heat oil over medium-high heat. Season chicken with salt and pepper. Working in batches, brown chicken on both sides. Place browned chicken in a 4- to 5-quart slow cooker. Add onions to slow cooker.

2. In a bowl, combine dark beer and barbecue sauce. Pour mixture over chicken and onions in slow cooker.

3. Cover and cook on high-heat setting for 3 to 4 hours or low-heat setting for 7 to 8 hours.

Apple-Raisin
Bread Pudding with
Cream Soda Sauce

servings 6 **prep time** 15 minutes
cooking time 3 hours (High)

Bread Pudding

2   packets (1.46 ounces each) cinnamon roll instant oatmeal, *Quaker Oats*®
3   eggs, beaten
3   cups milk, or 2 cups milk and 1 cup heavy cream
¼   cup brown sugar, *C&H*®
1½ teaspoons rum extract, *McCormick*®
½   teaspoon salt
3½ cups cubed raisin bread
1   cup apple pie filling or topping, *Comstock More Fruit*®
½   cup raisins, *Sun-Maid*®
    Nonstick cooking spray, *PAM*®

Sauce

½   cup cream soda
1   package (1.3-ounce) whipped topping mix, *Dream Whip*®
½   teaspoon ground cinnamon, *McCormick*®
½   teaspoon rum extract, *McCormick*®
½   teaspoon salt

1. For bread pudding, in a blender, blend instant oatmeal into a fine powder. Set aside.

2. In a large bowl, whisk together eggs, milk, brown sugar, rum extract, and salt. Fold in raisin bread, pie filling, raisins, and oatmeal powder until bread cubes are moist. Set aside for 30 minutes.

3. Spray a 3½- to 4-quart slow cooker with cooking spray. Add bread mixture. Cook on high-heat setting for 3 to 4 hours or until a knife inserted in center comes out clean.

4. For sauce, combine all sauce ingredients in a bowl. Whisk together until thickened. Top each bread pudding serving with a dollop of sauce and serve.

Hottie Sangría

servings 12 **prep time** 5 minutes
cooking time 1 hour (High)

- 2 bottles (750 ml) Rioja (Spanish red wine)
- 2 bottles (750 ml) white wine
- 2 cups frozen cherries
- 2 cups frozen peaches
- 1 cup simple syrup*
- 1 cup brandy, *Christian Brothers*®
- 1 orange, sliced
- 2 sticks cinnamon, *McCormick*®

1. Combine all ingredients in a 5- or 6-quart slow cooker.

2. Cover and heat on high-heat setting for 1 hour. Reduce to low-heat setting to maintain temperature. Ladle sangría into glasses. Be sure to include some fruit in each glass.

*Note: To make simple syrup, combine 1 cup sugar with 1 cup water in a saucepan. Bring to boil. Reduce heat and simmer for 5 minutes or until sugar is dissolved, stirring occasionally.

Hot Apple Cider Toddy

servings 4 **prep time** 5 minutes
cooking time 1 hour (High)

- 1 stick butter, softened
- ¼ cup light brown sugar, *C&H*®
- ½ teaspoon ground nutmeg, *McCormick*®
- ½ teaspoon ground cinnamon, *McCormick*®
- ½ teaspoon ground cloves, *McCormick*®
- 3 cups apple cider, *Welch's*®
- 1 cup bourbon, *Maker's Mark*®

1. In a bowl, combine butter, sugar, and spices. Whisk until butter becomes creamy and ingredients are incorporated. Roll butter mixture into 1-inch log. Wrap log in plastic wrap and refrigerate at least 1 hour.

2. Meanwhile, place apple cider in a 1- to 1½-quart slow cooker. Cover and heat on high-heat setting for 1 hour.

3. Pour 2 ounces bourbon in each of 4 mugs. Add hot cider to each mug and top with a slice of spiced butter.

Everyday Dinners

Cooking seven days a week can be downright daunting, even for those who look forward to doing it. Cooking both relaxes and stimulates me, helping me unwind after a busy day and rewarding me with a delicious meal as the fruit of my labors. But some days, I don't have the energy to spend one second more than I have to in the kitchen.

Every-night cooking is all about variety. This chapter offers fresh takes on everyday dishes, giving old standbys new appeal. You'll find meals for one and meals for many, speedy can-do dinners for Monday through Friday, and leisurely weekend suppers that invite the whole family to help. From Chicken Masala to Cornish game hens, you'll see how to make regional favorites the whole world loves, and pair them with side dishes that make meal planning a breeze. It's cooking at its quickest—everything you need to feed yourself and your loved ones all week long.

The Recipes

189

Corned Beef Hash with Poached Eggs

servings 6 **prep time** 10 minutes
cooking time 30 minutes

Corned Beef Hash

2   **tablespoons vegetable oil**
1/2   **cup thinly sliced red onion**
1½   **pounds deli corned beef, coarsely chopped**
1   **bag (32-ounce) frozen Southern-style hash browns, *Ore-Ida®***
2   **tablespoons Southwest steak marinade seasoning,**
     McCormick® Grill Mates®
1   **medium green bell pepper, sliced into ¼-inch strips**
1   **medium red bell pepper, sliced into ¼-inch strips**
1/2   **cup chopped green onions**
2   **tablespoons beef broth, *Swanson®***
     Dash Worcestershire sauce, *Lea & Perrins®*

Poached Eggs

1   **tablespoon white vinegar, *Heinz®***
6   **eggs**
6   **slices white bread, toasted**

1. For the hash, heat oil in a large skillet over medium heat. Add the red onion and cook until softened, about 3 minutes. Add corned beef, hash browns, steak marinade seasoning, peppers, green onions, broth, and Worcestershire sauce. Cook, stirring occasionally, until potatoes are golden and crisp, about 15 minutes.

2. For the eggs, fill a shallow skillet two-thirds full with water. Add vinegar. Place 6 medium biscuit cutters in water so they lay flat on the bottom of skillet. Bring to a simmer over low heat.

3. Break 1 egg and drop into a biscuit cutter. Repeat for remaining eggs. Simmer until eggs are poached, about 4 minutes. If desired, poach an additional 1 to 2 minutes until yolks are cooked through. Carefully remove eggs with spatula. Serve eggs and corned beef hash with toast.

Chicken Masala

servings 4 **prep time** 10 minutes
cooking time 30 minutes

- **4 boneless skinless chicken breast halves, rinsed and patted dry**
- 1/3 cup all-purpose flour
- 2 tablespoons canola oil, *Wesson*®
- 1 onion, chopped
- 1 teaspoon bottled minced garlic, *McCormick*®
- 1 can (14.5-ounce) diced tomatoes, drained, *Hunt's*®
- 1 cup light coconut milk
- 1/2 cup condensed cream of chicken soup, *Campbell's*®
- 1 tablespoon plus 2 teaspoons garam masala seasoning, *McCormick® Gourmet Collection*®

  Salt and pepper, to taste
- 1 cup frozen peas

  Plain or curried couscous

1. Place chicken breasts and flour in a resealable plastic bag; seal bag and toss to coat. Remove from bag and shake off excess flour. Set chicken aside.

2. In a large skillet, heat oil over medium-high heat. Brown chicken breasts on both sides. Remove to plate and set aside.

3. Add onion and garlic to skillet. Saute until soft. Add remaining ingredients, except the frozen peas, and stir to combine. Bring mixture to a boil. Reduce heat and return browned chicken to skillet. Simmer for 15 minutes.

4. Add frozen peas. Return to simmer and cook for 10 minutes more. Serve hot with plain or curried couscous.

Note: Garam masala is a traditional Indian blend of spices and is available in the spice section of the grocery store.

Hot Dates

servings 8 **prep time** 10 minutes
broiling time 5 minutes

- 1 can (15-ounce) pineapple chunks, drained, *Del Monte*®
- 1 package (8-ounce) pitted dates, *Sunsweet*®
- 1 package (16-ounce) bacon, slices cut in half, *Hormel*®

1. Preheat the broiler. Place a pineapple chunk inside each date. Wrap a half slice of bacon around each stuffed date and secure with toothpick. Place on a baking sheet.

2. Broil the dates 6 inches from heat source, turning occasionally, until bacon is crisp on all sides. Drain on paper towels. Serve warm.

Coffee-Crusted Beef Tenderloin

servings 6 **prep time** 5 minutes
stand time 1 hour + 25 minutes
roasting time 30 minutes

Complex in taste yet simple to make, this dinner du jour brims with café style. A dry rub of spiced ground coffee beans wakes up beef tenderloin and gives it a slightly crunchy crust. A masterful blend of flavors and textures—bittersweet coffee, sweet brown sugar, spicy paprika, and earthy sage—this coffee lover's dream is a special roast for special friends.

1   2-pound beef tenderloin, trimmed of fat and silver skin

Spice Rub
1/4   **cup finely ground coffee beans**
1/4   **cup brown sugar, *C&H*®**
2   **tablespoons chili powder, *McCormick*®**
2   **tablespoons paprika, *McCormick*®**
2   **teaspoons ground sage, *McCormick*®**
1   **teaspoon onion powder, *McCormick*®**
1/4   **teaspoon cayenne, *McCormick*®**
      Red onion, quartered

1. Remove meat from refrigerator 1 hour before roasting. Preheat oven to 500 degrees F. Fold over thin end of meat and tie with string.

2. In a small bowl, combine spice rub ingredients. Rub meat generously with the spice mixture. Let meat stand for 15 minutes and repeat rub.

3. Place meat on a rack in a roasting pan; arrange quartered red onions around meat. Do not cover. Place in oven. Turn oven down to 400 degrees F. Roast for 30 to 40 minutes, or until internal temperature of roast is 130 degrees F for rare to 145 degrees F for medium. Remove from oven; let meat rest for 10 minutes before slicing. Serve with Beef Coffee Gravy (below).

Beef Coffee Gravy

servings 6 **prep time** 2 minutes
cooking time 2 minutes

1   **can (15-ounce) beef broth, *Swanson*®**
1   **tablespoon Worcestershire sauce, *Lea & Perrins*®**
1   **teaspoon instant coffee crystals, *Maxwell House*®**
1/8   **teaspoon seasoned salt, *Lawry's*®**
2   **tablespoons cornstarch**
1/4   **cup water**
3   **tablespoons butter, cut into large chunks**
      Salt and pepper

1. In a medium saucepan, combine broth, Worcestershire sauce, coffee crystals, and seasoned salt and bring to boil. Reduce heat to simmer.

2. In a small bowl, dissolve the cornstarch in the water and whisk into broth mixture. Cook until gravy has thickened to the consistency of cream. Whisk in butter 1 chunk at a time. Season to taste with salt and pepper.

Sweet and Spicy Jerk-Glazed Game Hens

servings 4 **prep time** 10 minutes
roasting time 40 minutes

¼ cup frozen pineapple juice concentrate, thawed
1 tablespoon Jamaican jerk seasoning blend, ***McCormick® Gourmet Collection®***
2 tablespoons canola oil, ***Wesson®***
1 teaspoon salt
¼ teaspoon pepper
2 Cornish game hens, halved, rinsed, and patted dry

1. In a small bowl, combine all ingredients, except the hens. Put hens in a zip-top bag. Add marinade and seal bag. Turn bag to coat hens evenly. Refrigerate for 2 to 8 hours, turning bag occasionally.

2. Preheat oven to 400 degrees F. Remove hens from the marinade and place them, breast side up, in a roasting pan. Pour the remaining marinade over the hens. Roast for 40 to 45 minutes until golden.

Mushroom Salad in Cheese Crisps

servings 4 **prep time** 15 minutes
baking time 15 minutes

Olive oil nonstick cooking spray, ***PAM®***
1 container (7-ounce) shredded Parmesan, Romano, and Asiago cheese blend, ***Kraft®***
1½ cups baby spinach leaves
1 jar (4.5-ounce) whole mushrooms, ***Green Giant®***
1 cup halved cherry tomatoes
⅓ cup thinly sliced red onion
¼ cup Italian dressing

1. Preheat oven to 425 degrees F. Spray a baking sheet with cooking spray. Line baking sheet with parchment paper, then spray paper with cooking spray. Place ½ cup shredded cheese on half of the baking sheet and shape into a circle about 5 inches in diameter. Form a second circle on other half of baking sheet.

2. Bake about 5 minutes or until cheese is golden around edges. Using a wide spatula, carefully turn cheese rounds over. Bake about 2 minutes more or until deep golden around edges and set in the center. Using the spatula, carefully remove rounds and drape them over a large rolling pin suspended like a bridge between 2 tall cans. Let cool. Repeat with remaining cheese to make 2 more circles.

3. Meanwhile, combine spinach, mushrooms, tomatoes, and onion. Add dressing and toss to combine. To serve, place a cheese crisp on each of 4 salad plates, then top evenly with salad.

***Note:** Use the lid from a container of frozen whipped topping as a template for shaping the cheese crisps.

Steak Skewers

servings 4 **prep time** 5 minutes
marinate time 40 minutes **grilling time** 10 minutes

1   medium onion finely chopped
1/2   cup herb and garlic marinade, *Lawry's®*
1/4   cup ouzo (anise-flavored liqueur), *Metaxa®*
1/4   cup extra virgin olive oil, *Bertolli®*
1/3   cup chopped fresh mint
2   tablespoons brown sugar, *C&H®*
1½   teaspoons bottled minced garlic, *McCormick®*
       Salt and pepper to taste
1   pound top sirloin steak, cut into 1-inch cubes

1. In a large bowl, combine all ingredients, except steak. Add steak; place in refrigerator and marinate for 40 minutes. Drain and discard marinade. Thread steak cubes on skewers. Grill steak skewers over medium direct heat or broil 6 inches from heat for about 10 minutes, or until steak is desired doneness, turning skewers occasionally.

Goat Cheese Mashed Potatoes

servings 6 **prep time** 10 minutes
cooking time 10 minutes

2   pounds white potatoes, peeled and quartered
4   ounces goat cheese
4   tablespoons butter
3/4   to 1 cup evaporated milk, *Carnation®*
       Salt and white pepper

1. Place peeled and quartered potatoes in a large pot and cover with cold water. Bring to boil over medium-high heat. Reduce heat. Simmer until fork tender, about 10 to 15 minutes; drain.

2. Transfer potatoes to a large mixing bowl. With an electric mixer on low speed, break up potatoes. Add goat cheese, butter, and 1/2 cup evaporated milk. Whip potatoes on medium speed until smooth. Add evaporated milk to reach desired consistency. Season to taste with salt and white pepper.

Herbed Pork Roast and Creamy Mushroom Gravy

servings 8 **prep time** 15 minutes
baking time 1 hour **stand time** 10 minutes

Fast food doesn't necessarily come from a drive-thru window. With *Semi-Homemade®* you can whip up a wholesome home-cooked meal in less time than it takes to pick up takeout. A quartet of herbs subtly seasons the roast, while easy-to-make mushroom gravy pours on creamy goodness. It's a quick fix for every palate, a spur-of-the-moment meal made with minimal ingredients and maximum taste.

1　teaspoon minced fresh rosemary leaves, or ¼ teaspoon dried rosemary
1　teaspoon minced fresh parsley leaves, or ¼ teaspoon parsley flakes
1　teaspoon minced fresh thyme leaves, or ¼ teaspoon dried thyme leaves
1　tablespoon bottled minced garlic, *McCormick®*
1　2¹/₂- to 3-pound boneless pork loin roast
2　cans (10³/₄ ounces each) condensed cream of mushroom soup (98% fat-free), *Campbell's®*
1　cup skim milk

1. Preheat oven to 325 degrees F. Combine herbs and garlic. Cut small slits over surface of roast and press herb mixture into slits. Place roast on a rack in a roasting pan; do not cover. Place in oven and roast until the internal temperature is 165 degrees F. Remove roast from pan and let rest 10 minutes.

2. Stir soup into drippings in roasting pan and heat over medium heat. Gradually stir in skim milk. Continue to stir until mixture boils. Remove from heat. Slice roast and serve with gravy.

Rib-Eye with Chocolate-Spice Sauce

servings 2 **prep time** 5 minutes
cooking time 30 minutes
stand time 5 minutes

1   **cup meat-flavored pasta sauce,** *Prego*®
1   **cup low-sodium beef broth,** *Swanson*®
¼   **cup red wine**
1   **ounce semisweet chocolate,** *Nestlé*®
½   **teaspoon pumpkin pie spice,** *McCormick*®
¼   **teaspoon red pepper flakes,** *McCormick*®
2   **rib-eye steaks, 1 inch thick**
     Salt and pepper
2   **tablespoons unsalted butter**

1. In a medium saucepan, combine pasta sauce, broth, wine, chocolate, pumpkin pie spice, and red pepper flakes. Bring to a boil over medium-high heat, stirring occasionally. Reduce heat to low; simmer sauce for 30 minutes.

2. Meanwhile, season steaks generously on both sides with salt and pepper, patting the seasoning into the meat.

3. Heat a large heavy skillet, preferably cast iron, over medium heat. Add butter to hot skillet. When melted, add the steaks and cook until seared and well-crusted on 1 side, about 4 minutes. Turn and cook 3 minutes more for medium-rare and 4 minutes more for medium.

4. Transfer steaks to cutting board and let rest for 5 minutes, covered loosely with foil. Place steaks on plate, and spoon sauce over top.

Baked Pork Chops with Sweet Potatoes and Pears

servings 4 **prep time** 15 minutes
baking time 30 minutes

4 cans (15 ounces each) cut sweet potatoes, drained, *Princella*®
3 pears, peeled, quartered, and cored
⅓ cup chopped pecans
⅓ cup brown sugar, packed, *C&H*®
3 tablespoons plus ½ cup all-purpose flour
3 tablespoons butter, melted
Olive oil nonstick cooking spray, *PAM*®
2 eggs, beaten
1 cup Italian seasoned bread crumbs, *Progresso*®
1 tablespoon herbes de Provence, *McCormick*® *Gourmet Collection*®
4 bone-in pork loin chops, ¾ inch thick

1. Preheat oven to 350 degrees F. In an 8-inch square baking dish, combine sweet potatoes and pears. In a small bowl, combine pecans, brown sugar, 3 tablespoons flour, and the butter to make a paste. Crumble mixture over potatoes and pears. Set aside.

2. Spray a roasting pan and rack with cooking spray. Place eggs in a shallow bowl. Place ½ cup flour on a plate. Place bread crumbs and herbes de Provence on another plate and mix well. Dredge pork chops in flour. Dip in eggs, then in bread crumb mixture, coating pork. Arrange chops on rack in prepared pan and coat lightly with cooking spray.

3. Bake pork chops alongside sweet potatoes and pears for 20 to 30 minutes, or until chops are cooked to desired doneness and sweet potatoes and pears are tender.

Brandied Bananas

servings 4 **prep time** 10 minutes
cooking time 10 minutes

4   **bananas**
2   **tablespoons butter**
3   **tablespoons brown sugar, *C&H*®**
½   **teaspoon ground cinnamon, *McCormick*®**
½   **cup tequila, *Jose Cuervo Especial*®**
1   **tablespoon brandy, *Christian Brothers*®**
      Vanilla or coconut ice cream

1. Peel bananas and cut each in half crosswise, then cut each half in half again lengthwise. In a large skillet, melt butter over low heat. Place bananas in skillet, cut sides down, and cook for 5 minutes. Turn and cook for 5 minutes more. Sprinkle with sugar and cinnamon. Transfer bananas to a heatproof serving dish and arrange in a single layer. Pour tequila and brandy into same skillet and heat over medium heat, scraping any browned bits up with spatula.

2. When mixture is hot, use a long match to carefully ignite mixture in pan, then pour over bananas. When flames die down, place 4 banana pieces on each of four dessert dishes. Top with scoops of ice cream and spoon sauce over ice cream.

Custard Cream Pound Cake

servings 4 **prep time** 10 minutes
cooking time 10 minutes

1   **package (3-ounce) flan mix, *Jell-O*®**
2   **cups milk**
½   **cup Marsala wine**
1   **16-ounce frozen pound cake, thawed, *Sara Lee*®**
1   **package (16-ounce) frozen peach slices, thawed but not drained**
      Ground nutmeg, *McCormick*®

1. Remove caramel sauce packet from flan box and set aside for another use. Using 2 cups milk, prepare custard according to the flan package directions. Stir in wine. Cool for 15 minutes.

2. Cut cake into 8 equal slices. Overlap 2 slices on each dessert plate. Top cake with 4 or 5 peach slices and 1 to 2 tablespoons of the peach juice. Spoon about ⅓ cup custard sauce over the peaches, then sprinkle with nutmeg.

Boston Cream Cupcakes

servings 12 **prep time** 20 minutes
chill time 15 minutes + 1 hour

1¼ cups cold whole milk
1 box (3.4-ounce) vanilla instant pudding and pie filling mix, *Jell-O®*
1 tablespoon pure vanilla extract, *McCormick®*
12 premade cupcakes, baked from a cake mix
1 cup heavy cream
1 package (12-ounce) semisweet chocolate morsels, *Nestlé®*
¼ cup powdered sugar, sifted, *C&H®*

1. For filling, combine milk, instant pudding mix, and vanilla in a large bowl. Beat mixture for 2 minutes or until it thickens. Refrigerate filling for 15 minutes. Spoon filling into a pastry bag fitted with a medium plain tip. Fill cupcakes by inserting tip into tops of cupcakes and squeezing a couple of tablespoons of filling into each cupcake.

2. For ganache, heat heavy cream in a small heavy saucepan over medium heat until steaming. (Do not boil.) Remove saucepan from heat and add chocolate morsels; stir with a whisk until smooth. Spoon, drizzle, or spread ganache over cupcakes or dunk cupcake tops into ganache. Refrigerate for 1 hour before serving.

Metropolitini

servings 1
prep time 2 minutes

Ice cubes
1½ **ounces gin,** *Tanqueray®*
1½ **ounces bourbon,** *Maker's Mark®*
½ **ounce orange-flavored liqueur,** *Cointreau®*
Maraschino cherry

1. Fill a cocktail shaker with ice cubes and add gin, bourbon, and Cointreau. Shake well. Strain into a martini glass. Garnish with a cherry.

Kimbo Mojito

servings 1
prep time 5 minutes

1 **lime, cut in quarters**
Ice
1 **shot white rum,** *Havana Club®*
1 **shot liquid sugar**
6 **fresh mint leaves, minced**
Splash club soda, *Canada Dry®*
Sugar cane stick, for garnish
Fresh mint sprigs, for garnish

1. Squeeze lime wedges into a cocktail shaker filled with ice. Add squeezed limes to shaker. Add rum, liquid sugar, and mint leaves. Shake vigorously for 20 seconds.

2. Pour into highball glass and top with a splash of club soda. Garnish with sugar cane stick and fresh mint sprigs.

Special Occasions

As much as I look forward to an intimate evening with family and friends, I'm the first to enjoy a lively crowd. Two's company; three's a party. The more the merrier rings true when you plan can't-go-wrong dishes that serve up great taste with a small helping of time and effort.

When it comes to entertaining, easy does it best. This chapter is an elegant, yet practical, resource for occasion cooking, filled with simple year-round and seasonal favorites that are as appealing to the eye as they are to the palate. You can make some ahead to save time, for instance, prime rib or ham, while others, such as one-pot pastas and hors d'oeuvres, pull together right before company arrives. Whether you're entertaining for every day, a special day, or the holidays, keeping it creative is the recipe for a good time for both you and your guests.

The Recipes

Lox and Cream Cheese-Stuffed Cucumbers

makes 4 **prep time** 20 minutes
cooking time 5 minutes

- 2 unwaxed cucumbers
- 1 container (8-ounce) cream cheese, softened, *Philadelphia*®
- 1 container (8-ounce) sour cream
- 1 (3-ounce) package lox or smoked salmon, chopped into small pieces
- 1 shallot, diced
- 1/2 lemon, juiced, seeds removed
- Pinch salt and freshly ground pepper
- Fresh dill sprigs, for garnish

1. Using a peeler, create stripes on the outside of the cucumbers by peeling along lengths of cucumbers, leaving every other section intact. Cut off ends of cucumbers and slice into 1-inch rounds. Using a melon baller, scoop out the seeds and flesh from the top two-thirds of each round. (Do not scoop all the way through.) Set aside.

2. In a medium bowl, combine cream cheese and sour cream. Stir in salmon, shallot, lemon juice, salt, and pepper. Transfer to a pastry bag fitted with a large star tip*. Pipe filling generously into cucumber rounds. Garnish each round with a dill sprig.

*Tip: If you don't own a pastry bag, follow the instructions in the recipe above to use a resealable plastic bag to pipe filling.

Deviled Eggs

makes 24 **prep time** 25 minutes
cooking time 12 minutes

- 12 eggs
- 4 tablespoons mayonnaise, *Best Foods*®
- 2 teaspoons yellow mustard, *French's*®
- 2 teaspoons sweet pickle relish, *Del Monte*®
- Salt and pepper
- Paprika, for dusting

1. Place eggs in a large saucepan and cover with cold water. Bring to a gentle boil, and boil for 12 minutes. Remove eggs from water; cool in refrigerator. Peel eggs and slice in half lengthwise. Separate egg yolks and place in a bowl. Place whites on a separate plate.

2. Add mayonnaise, mustard, relish, and salt and pepper to taste to yolks; mash together with a fork until creamy and smooth. Spoon yolk mixture into a pastry bag or a resealable plastic bag. To use plastic bag as a pastry bag, cut 1 corner off to make a 1/4-inch diameter opening and fit with a large star tip. Pipe yolk mixture into egg white halves. Dust tops with paprika. Refrigerate. Serve cold.

"These are the best deviled eggs you will ever eat." – Sandra

French Bean Casserole

servings 6 **prep time** 15 minutes
baking time 20 minutes

- 1 tablespoon olive oil, *Bertolli®*
- 1 small onion, minced
- 6 ounces crimini mushrooms, sliced
- 1 can (10³/₄-ounce) condensed cream of mushroom soup, *Campbell's®*
- 1 cup heavy cream
- 1 pound baby green beans, trimmed and cleaned
- ¹/₂ cup toasted almonds

1. Preheat oven to 350 degrees F. In a medium skillet over medium heat, heat oil. Add onion and saute until soft. Stir in mushrooms. Increase heat to medium-high and saute until mushrooms are golden and most of the moisture has evaporated.

2. Stir in soup and cream. Cook and stir until simmering. Stir in the green beans. Pour mixture into a buttered 9×13-inch baking dish and top with toasted almonds. Bake for 20 to 25 minutes or until beans are tender.

White Wine Fondue

servings 6 **prep time** 10 minutes
cooking time 10 minutes

- 2 tablespoons butter
- 2 tablespoons all-purpose flour
- 1 cup white wine
- 1 cup whole milk
- ¹/₂ teaspoon garlic salt, *McCormick®*
- 1 can (10³/₄-ounce) cheddar cheese soup, *Campbell's®*
- 1¹/₂ cups shredded Swiss cheese

1. In a medium skillet over medium-high heat, melt butter. Whisk in flour. Cook the flour-butter mixture (called a roux) to a blond color, whisking constantly.

2. Whisk in the wine and let reduce by half. Whisk in the milk and garlic salt. Whisk in the soup. Add cheese and continue to whisk until melted.

Serving Idea: Serve fondue with cubed bread, gherkins, baby carrots, blanched broccoli, cooked potatoes, and Little Smokies®.

Chive Roasted Potatoes with Horseradish-Sour Cream and Caviar

servings 12 **prep time** 25 minutes **cooking time** 35 minutes

- 2 **pounds new red potatoes, or a mixture of red and purple potatoes**
- 2 **tablespoons extra virgin olive oil, *Bertolli*®**
- 2 **tablespoons finely chopped fresh chives**
- 1/2 **teaspoon Kosher salt**
- 1/4 **teaspoon pepper**
- 1/2 **cup sour cream**
- 1 **teaspoon prepared horseradish, *Morehouse*®**
- 1 **jar (2-ounce) caviar**

1. Preheat oven to 400 degrees F. Line a baking sheet with parchment paper. Rinse potatoes and pat dry with paper towels. Slice into 1/2-inch rounds. Place in a medium bowl and drizzle with oil. Add chives, salt, and pepper; toss to coat.

2. Arrange potatoes in a single layer on prepared baking sheet. Roast for 35 to 40 minutes or until potatoes are tender. Remove from oven and let cool.

3. In a small bowl, combine sour cream and horseradish. Top each roasted potato round with a dollop of sour cream mixture. With a plastic spoon (do not use a metal spoon for caviar), add a small amount of caviar to each dollop of sour cream. Serve at room temperature.

Candied Yam Soufflé

servings 8 **prep time** 20 minutes **baking time** 30 minutes

- 1 **stick butter**
- 1 **cup light brown sugar, *C&H*®**
- 1/2 **cup chopped pecans**
- 4 **cans (15 ounces each) large sweet potatoes, drained, *Princella*®**
- 1 **teaspoon ground cinnamon, *McCormick*®**
- 1 **teaspoon ground nutmeg, *McCormick*®**
- 1 **jar (13-ounce) marshmallow topping**

1. Preheat oven to 325 degrees F. In a saucepan over medium heat, melt butter. Stir in brown sugar and pecans. Simmer for 3 minutes.

2. Meanwhile, place sweet potatoes in a large bowl and mash with a potato masher (leaving some chunked pieces). Pour sugar mixture over sweet potatoes. Add cinnamon and nutmeg. Stir until thoroughly combined. Transfer to a metal pie pan. Top with marshmallow topping.

3. Bake for 15 minutes. Remove from oven. To brown the top, raise oven temperature to 400 degrees F and bake for 10 minutes more. Do not overbrown.

Pumpkin Ravioli
in Brown Butter

servings 8 to 10 **prep time** 25 minutes
cooking time 10 minutes

This discriminating dish is like a perfect party guest: Keep it circulating and the crowd stays happy. Ground nutmeg brings out the pumpkin's sweetness, an aromatic contrast with pungent onion and rich ricotta and Parmesan cheeses. The bright orange filling is a surprise sure to make these stylish sweeties a conversation piece, whether they're mingling at a dinner party or on the family dinner table.

1   **stick butter**
2   cups canned pumpkin, *Libby's®*
1   packet (0.7-ounce) onion recipe mix, *Lipton® Carb Options™*
1   cup vegetable broth, *Swanson®*
        Salt and pepper
¼   cup low-fat ricotta cheese, *Precious®*
3   tablespoons grated Parmesan cheese, *Kraft®*
1   teaspoon ground nutmeg, *McCormick®*
16   wonton wrappers, *Melissa's®*
10   fresh sage leaves
2   tablespoons grated Parmesan cheese, for garnish, *Kraft®*

1. For filling, in a large saucepan over medium heat, melt 1 tablespoon of the butter. Add pumpkin, onion recipe mix, and broth; simmer 5 minutes. Continue cooking until mixture is slightly dry. Season to taste with salt and pepper and remove from heat. Stir in ricotta cheese, 3 tablespoons Parmesan cheese, and the nutmeg. Let cool completely.

2. Place 1 teaspoon of pumpkin filling in center of wonton wrapper. Fold wrapper diagonally to form a triangle. Moisten the edges of the triangle to seal. Using a fork, press down on the folded edge. Repeat. Place raviolis in a pot of boiling water and cook until they float to the top. Drain well.

3. In a large skillet over medium heat, melt remaining 7 tablespoons butter. Add sage leaves. Cook until butter turns brown. Arrange raviolis on a platter and spoon brown butter over top. Sprinkle with 2 tablespoons Parmesan cheese.

Crown Roast with Sourdough Dressing

servings 10 to 12 **prep time** 30 minutes
baking time 2½ hours

Crown Roast

5 tablespoons Worcestershire sauce, *Lea & Perrins®*
1 packet (1.2-ounce) green peppercorn marinade mix, *McCormick®*
1 packet (1-ounce) zesty herb seasoning mix, *McCormick® Grill Mates®*
1 7- to 8-pound pork crown roast

Sourdough Dressing

4 hot Italian sausages, casings removed
1 packet (0.9-ounce) onion mushroom soup mix, *Lipton®*
1 can (16-ounce) fat-free, low-sodium chicken broth, *Swanson®*
1 can (10-ounce) condensed golden mushroom soup, *Campbell's®*
6 cups sourdough croutons
⅓ cup fresh Italian parsley leaves, chopped
1 teaspoon dried thyme, *McCormick®*
1 teaspoon dried marjoram, *McCormick®*
   Salt and pepper

1. Preheat the oven to 325 degrees F.

2. For crown roast, in a shallow roasting pan, combine the Worcestershire sauce, green peppercorn marinade mix, and herb seasoning mix. Place crown roast, bone ends up, in pan. Wrap bone ends with aluminum foil to prevent them from browning too quickly. Using a pastry brush or spoon, coat the entire meat surface with the sauce mixture. Transfer the pan to the oven and roast, uncovered, for 20 to 25 minutes per pound of meat (2½ to 3½ hours).

3. For sourdough dressing, in a large nonstick skillet over medium heat, brown the sausages. Add the onion mushroom soup mix, broth, and soup. Stir in croutons, parsley, thyme, and marjoram. Season to taste with salt and pepper.

4. Remove roast from oven about 45 minutes before it is done. Fill the cavity with sourdough dressing. Return roast to oven and cook for remaining 45 minutes. Transfer roast to a platter and remove foil from bone ends.

Note: Bake any extra stuffing in a separate dish alongside roast for remaining 45 minutes.

Bourbon Honey-Glazed Ham

servings 10 to 12 **prep time** 15 minutes
cooking time 1 hour **stand time** 20 minutes

1	cup clover honey, *Sue Bee*®
²/₃	cup bourbon or other whiskey
½	cup orange marmalade (100% fruit), *Smuckers*®
⅓	cup molasses
1	5-pound whole bone-in smoked ham, fully cooked
⅛	cup whole cloves, *McCormick*®

1. Preheat oven to 350 degrees F.

2. In a medium saucepan over low heat, heat honey, bourbon, marmalade, and molasses for 15 minutes or until reduced by half, stirring occasionally. Set aside.

3. With a sharp knife, cut a diamond pattern into the fatty part of the ham. Stud whole cloves in each diamond at points where lines cross. Spread half of the bourbon glaze over the ham. Roast, uncovered, for 30 minutes. Baste occasionally with remaining glaze and continue to roast for another 15 minutes. Let ham stand for 20 minutes before slicing.

Tip: When measuring honey and molasses, spray measuring cup with nonstick cooking spray to easily remove them from cup.

Goat Cheese Polenta

servings 4 **prep time** 10 minutes
cooking time 15 minutes

2	tablespoons butter
1	package (24-ounce) precooked polenta, *San Gennaro*®
1	cup half-and-half or light cream
4	ounces goat cheese
1	tablespoon finely chopped fresh tarragon
	Salt and pepper

1. In a saucepan over medium heat, melt butter. Break polenta into small pieces and add to pan. Whisk in half-and-half and continue stirring until smooth and heated through.

2. Add goat cheese and tarragon to polenta. Whisk until goat cheese is melted. Season to taste with salt and pepper.

Herb Salt-Crusted Prime Rib

servings 4 **prep time** 15 minutes
baking time 50 minutes

1   3½-pound beef rib roast (ribs removed)
¼   cup Worcestershire sauce, *Lea & Perrins®*
1   tablespoon seasoned pepper (salt free), *Lawry's®*
4   pounds Kosher salt
1   packet (1.12-ounce) Italian herb marinade mix, *Durkee® Grill Creations®*
½   cup water
1   can (14-ounce) low-sodium beef broth, *Swanson®*
1   packet (0.9-ounce) onion soup mix, *Lipton®*

1. Preheat oven to 500 degrees F. Line a roasting pan with aluminum foil. Sprinkle roast with Worcestershire sauce and seasoned pepper.

2. In a medium bowl, combine kosher salt and herb marinade mix. Sprinkle water over salt mixture until salt is well-moistened but not wet. Spread a ½-inch layer of salt mixture in middle of roasting pan, making it slightly larger than the diameter of the roast. Place roast, fat side up, on top of salt layer. Insert oven-safe meat thermometer into center of roast. Carefully pat remaining salt mixture onto meat, covering roast completely.

3. Place roast in oven and reduce temperature to 425 degrees F. Roast, uncovered, for 14 to 16 minutes per pound or until thermometer reads 5 degrees less than desired temperature. (Final temperature for rare will be 130 degrees F, 135 degrees F for medium-rare, or 140 degrees F for medium.) Remove roast from oven and let rest for 5 minutes.

4. For jus, in a small saucepan over medium heat, bring broth to boil. Reduce heat, add soup mix, and simmer for 5 minutes. Remove from heat. To serve, remove salt crust from roast by breaking and peeling (you may need a hammer for this). Slice roast and transfer slices to a platter. Ladle a small amount of jus over meat and serve remaining jus on the side.

Tip: Have butcher remove ribs from roast.

Sour Cream Mashed Potatoes

servings 6 **prep time** 10 minutes
cooking time 10 minutes

2   pounds white potatoes, peeled and quartered
4   ounces sour cream
4   tablespoons butter
¾   to 1 cup buttermilk
       Salt and white pepper

1. Place potatoes in large pot and cover with cold water. Bring to boil. Reduce heat and simmer until fork tender, 10 to 15 minutes; drain. Transfer potatoes to a large bowl. With electric mixer on low speed, break up potatoes. Add sour cream, butter, and ½ cup buttermilk. Whip potatoes on medium speed until smooth. Add buttermilk to reach desired consistency. Season to taste with salt and pepper.

Turkey with Cornbread Stuffing and Gravy

servings 8 to 10
prep time 45 minutes
baking time 4 hours
stand time 15 minutes

- 1 **12-pound turkey, thawed**
- 1 **box (8.5-ounce) cornbread mix,** *Jiffy*®
- 1 **cup chopped celery**
- ½ **cup chopped green onions**
- 2 **tablespoons poultry seasoning,** *McCormick*®
- 1 **can (10.5-ounce) chicken with rice soup,** *Campbell's*®
- 1 **stick butter, softened**
- 3 **tablespoons vegetable oil**
- 3 **tablespoons all-purpose flour**
- **Salt and pepper**

1. Rinse the turkey in clean water and pat dry with paper towels. Remove the gizzards and neck. Place gizzards and neck in a saucepan and cover with water. Bring to a simmer to create broth for gravy. Simmer for 30 to 45 minutes. Remove from heat, strain, and reserve.

2. Meanwhile, prepare cornbread according to package directions. Crumble cornbread into small pieces and lay on a baking sheet to air dry. In a bowl, combine prepared cornbread, celery, and green onions. Add poultry seasoning and soup. Mix well; stuff inside turkey cavities.

3. Generously cover turkey with softened butter. Tent with aluminum foil and bake according to package instructions for bird's weight. One hour before bird is done, remove foil and baste. The turkey is done when the internal temperature registers 170 degrees F deep in the thigh and juices run clear when flesh is pierced. The temperature of the stuffing should be 160 degrees F in the center.

4. Remove turkey from oven, place on a serving platter, and tent with foil. Let turkey rest for about 15 minutes so the temperature of the stuffing will reach 165 degrees F in the center and the temperature in the thigh will rise to 180 degrees F.

5. While turkey rests, prepare gravy. In a large skillet over medium-low heat, heat the oil. Add flour; cook and stir until deep brown. Add turkey drippings and whisk until thickened. Add reserved gizzard broth and simmer. Season with to taste with salt and pepper.

6. Remove stuffing from bird and place in serving bowl. Carve turkey and plate with stuffing and gravy.

Kahlua® Soufflés

servings 6 **prep time** 15 minutes
baking time 20 minutes

People hear the word "soufflé" and their face falls. I thought soufflés were temperamental, too, until I came up with this foolproof recipe. It's an after-dinner drink and dessert in one, a melt-in-your-mouth medley of sweet chocolate, velvety Kahlua®, and deep, dark espresso. Serve in individual ramekins for a fuss-free finale to an elegant evening. If—by chance—your soufflés should fall, you'll have the most brilliant soufflé brownies ever!

1	cup semisweet chocolate morsels, *Nestlé®*
¹⁄₂	cup *Kahlua®* (coffee-flavored liqueur)
5	eggs
1	package (8-ounce) cream cheese, cubed, *Philadelphia®*
	Unsalted butter
	Sugar, *C&H®*
1	tablespoon powdered sugar, *C&H®*
1	teaspoon instant coffee crystals or espresso powder

1. Preheat oven to 350 degrees F. In a small saucepan, combine chocolate morsels and Kahlua®. Heat over very low heat until chocolate is melted, stirring to blend. Remove from heat and cool slightly.

2. Place eggs in blender and blend well. With the blender on, slowly pour cooled chocolate mixture through lid opening. Add cream cheese, a few cubes at a time, and blend until smooth.

3. Pour into 6 buttered and sugared 6-ounce ramekins or ovenproof custard cups*. Place ramekins on a baking sheet.

4. Bake for 20 minutes or until edges are set but centers are still slightly soft. (If desserts were refrigerated, bake for 5 minutes longer.) Combine powdered sugar and coffee crystals. As soon as soufflés are done, remove from oven, place each on a dessert plate, and sift some sugar mixture through sieve over of each soufflé. Serve immediately.

***Tip:** At this point, desserts can be covered and refrigerated for several hours until ready to bake.

Special Occasions | 233

Holiday Champagne

servings 1 **prep time** 10 minutes

- 1 part champagne, chilled, *Korbel®*
- 1 part cranberry juice, chilled
  Fresh cranberries, for garnish
  Bamboo skewers, for garnish

1. Fill a champagne flute halfway with chilled cranberry juice; fill the rest of the flute with champagne (adjust to your preference). Garnish with cranberry stir stick.

2. For cranberry stir stick, trim a bamboo skewer to 1 inch longer than the flute. Thread with cranberries; place in flute.

Strawberry Star Champagne

servings 1 **prep time** 2 minutes

- 1 part strawberry-kiwi juice, chilled, *Kern's®*
- 1 part champagne, chilled, *Korbel®*

1. Pour strawberry-kiwi juice into a champagne flute. Add champagne and stir.

Peach Perfect Champagne

servings 1 **prep time** 3 minutes

- 1 part peach juice, chilled, *Kern's®*
- 1 part champagne, chilled, *Korbel®*

1. Pour peach juice into champagne flute. Add champagne and stir.

Lemon Champagne

servings 1 **prep time** 3 minutes

- 1 part frozen lemonade concentrate
- 1 part champagne, chilled, *Korbel®*

1. In a large pitcher, combine lemonade concentrate and chilled champagne. Stir and serve.

Pink Lemonade Champagne

servings 8 to 10 **prep time** 5 minutes

- 1 can (12-ounce) frozen pink lemonade concentrate
- 2 bottles champagne, chilled, *Korbel®*

1. In a large pitcher, combine pink lemonade concentrate and chilled champagne. Stir and serve.

UNICEF Snowflake Cocktail

servings 4 **prep time** 5 minutes

  White sugar crystals
- 2 cups store-bought eggnog, chilled
- ½ cup brandy, *Christian Brothers®*
- ½ cup almond-flavored liqueur, *Amaretto di Saronno®*
- ½ cup vanilla ice cream
- 1 teaspoon ground nutmeg, *McCormick®*
  Pumpkin pie spice, for garnish, *McCormick®*

1. Rim martini glasses with sugar crystals. Combine eggnog, brandy, amaretto, ice cream, and nutmeg in a blender; blend until smooth. Pour into glasses. Garnish each cocktail with a pinch of pumpkin pie spice.

From left to right: Peach Perfect Champagne; Strawberry Star Champagne; and Lemon Champagne; Holiday Champagne; Pink Lemonade Champagne.
On the left: UNICEF Snowflake Cocktail

Index

Index (cont.)

239

Free

Lifestyle web magazine subscription

Just visit **www.semi-homemade.com** today to subscribe!

Each issue is filled with new, easy how-to projects, simple lifestyle tips, and an abundance of helpful hints. For busy people on a budget and on-the-go, the Semi-Homemade® Magazine is the perfect way to have it all.

fabulous florals

gifts & giving

semi-homemaker's tips & tricks

home & garden

entertaining & gatherings

music & movies

fashion & beauty

perfect parties

marvelous meals

tables & settings

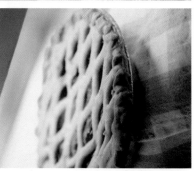